How to Make African Countries Stable

Bangne Plan

By
Abel Bangne

I dedicate my book to those proud African people who are dying of starvation, diseases, and civil war in Africa because of the greed, incompetence, ignorance, weakness, and lack of passion, love and vision of their so called leaders. These leaders are prepared to do anything imaginable to be in power.

How to Make African Countries Stable

Bangne Plan

I would like to use this opportunity to tell my proud fellow African people they do not have to be humiliated, exploited and suffer at the hands of their so-called leaders because the real power is in their hands – the hands of the people. In each country, African people must stand together as one people, put aside their differences (religious, ethnic, or tribal/caste groups) and fight together for the interests, stability, peace and progress of their countries. If each religious, ethnic, tribal or caste group wants to fight their individual and selfish battles, then no one will win, everybody will lose. African people cannot afford to lose the battle for their freedom and well-being. Our children, grandchildren and great-grandchildren must have a better life than us, and not become slaves like us. African people must do anything in their power to achieve stability and peace in their respective countries. Doing nothing, not willing to make the ultimate sacrifices, we Africans of this 21st century will be responsible for what will happen to the life of our children and grandchildren and the next generation. We Africans must conquer our fear – death. Death must never and should never scare you. It's how you will die that must scare you. You do not want to die humiliated without any honour and dignity in your own country. You do not want to die with your tail between your legs. When your time comes, you have to die with pride, dignity and honour for your country. Fight to protect the integrity, the interest and unity of your country, not destroy it.

Most African leaders simply do not care about their people; they benefit from people's divisions and are prepared to sacrifice the lives of the people they are supposed to save to achieve their goal. Most of our leaders take advantage of a divided population in order to succeed in their quest for power. United, Africans can live like Westerners. Divided, Africans will live like 'savages' for many generations. The choice is ours. On which side do we want to be? Do we want to fight as one and live together in stable, prosperous, united and peaceful countries? Or do we want to fight against each other and live in countries torn apart by conflict, diseases, starvation, corruption and vices?

How can you support, tolerate, follow and defend any political leader who uses religion or ethnic division as a policy, as a programme to govern?

The day African people will conquer their fear of death, they will be FREE.

Free from tyranny, dictatorship and slavery.

Any race that is not prepared to die for its freedom and independence will be dominated, tamed and suffer slavery.

Thank you, God, for making most African lands fertile. Unfortunately that fertility attracted a lot of predators. These predators came as missionaries. They discovered the wealth, conquered the land, and made the natives slaves (mentally, physically, and financially). After they stripped our land of most of its natural resources in the name of God, they decided to go back where they came from (Europe).

Thank you, God: finally Africans thought they were free; they naively thought they could taste the air of freedom. They thought they could now choose their own leaders – leaders who know what it is to be slaves, leaders who know what it is to be tortured, humiliated, and robbed of their dignity. We Africans put our faith in the hands of these leaders to make us proud; to purify our souls; to give us democracy, freedom, and justice for all; to take us out of misery. We refuse to be slaves again and are ready to die if necessary so that we can keep our freedom.

Thank you, God: Despite the massive exploitation of our land, we still have some wealth we could use to provide a better future for ourselves, our children, and our grandchildren. With that remaining wealth we could provide stability, decent housing, healthcare, education, and jobs for everyone. Unfortunately, my Lord, we Africans are still not free; we are still slaves. Our leaders whom we trusted have become worse than our predators. Our leaders who were supposed to free us became our masters. Our leaders are so cruel to us, we Africans are begging our 'predators' to allow us into their countries so that we can work and provide better conditions for our families in Africa.

What are we going to do? Should we sit around doing nothing? Should we just watch our countries being torn apart by war, starvation, and disease, caused by our own corrupt leaders with the help of their Western allies? We Africans must refuse to be slaves again. We must refuse to be exploited by anyone, no matter who they are (our own people or foreigners). Should you sit around doing nothing and watch your people begging for mercy to live in their own country? African people, freedom and independence were taken away by force. African people must take back their freedom and independence, by force if necessary. The continent was colonized and exploited by the West who now control African governments with an iron fist. The more unstable, the more chaotic African countries become, the easier it is for the Western countries to have their iron claw on all our natural resources. Natural resources which Western countries desperately needed to 'feed' their economies to make their countries 'big', powerful, dominant and strong. While European countries are stronger and more modern, African countries are going backwards to the stone age. The people of each African country must stand up as one to have any hope for their freedom, for the sake of the stability of their motherland, or they will be fighting a lost cause. Together as a unit, we are unbreakable and powerful; but divided, we are invisible and voiceless.

The whole world is laughing at us. The world does not understand how a continent as rich as Africa with vast natural resources, has the poorest population on this planet. Technology and science can be taught and learned, but natural resources cannot just be created, no matter how advanced your technology and science may be.

In October 2007, an American scientist, a winner of the Nobel Prize for Medicine for his part in discovering the molecular structure of DNA, stated he strongly believed that African people are less intelligent than Westerners. He also said Black employees are difficult to work with. These comments were published on the internet and in many newspapers in England and the rest of the European countries.

The American scientist mentioned is not just any scientist. He is one of the pioneers of DNA research and worked for many years as director of the Cold Spring Laboratory on Long Island (USA), which is a world-leading establishment in cancer and genetics research. We all know it is not true. God gave all human beings, whatever race they are – Blacks, Whites, or Asians – the same intelligence and the same ability. Within every race we can find intelligent people as well as very stupid people. What I can say is that the American scientist is one of the intelligent people of his race, who used his position to express his racist views using supposed scientific justification. What intrigues me is that if someone respects that American scientist for his scientific achievements, would they be influenced by his racial theories?

It is true that most of the African countries were colonized, exploited, and left on the verge of bankruptcy in the hands of corrupt leaders by the West. Many African countries have great wealth in terms of natural resources, and some have a perfect climate for agriculture to feed their people. Unfortunately, people see little improvement in their daily lives. People are always hungry, live in poor housing, drink filthy water, are forced to pay high prices for fuel, and cannot afford education. All the while, their so-called leaders and their closest relatives and friends fill their own bank accounts and send their children to the best schools in Europe.

Message to African leaders:

African leaders, for your ego you make the nation believe, you make the all world believe that you love your people and your people love you. The images displayed on your national TV can prove that: After a long trip abroad, you bribe a lot of people who come to the airport, your poor people who queue on the road all day under the heat of the sun to welcome you. After welcoming you, after clapping their hands so hard they can bleed just to make you happy, smile. After singing your name as the greatest of all, as a god, your people go home, then the reality of their miserable life sinks in (no money for food, to pay their bills, to pay for medication, and they watch their children starve all day).

The same people who were singing your name as the greatest of all, will be cursing you as their president. The same people will curse you and your government every day, will blame you and your government for not doing enough to improve their life. These people will blame you because while they struggle every day to make ends meet, you, their president and your closest friends and their families have a beautiful life where everything they desire is offered to them.

What will happen tomorrow when your Western allies who protect you, decide to replace you by somebody else then leave you to the vendetta of your own people?

The same people who were clapping their hands, who were singing your name to welcome you after every trip abroad will turn against you, your family, your closest allies and their family for revenge and revenge. The people will get it.

Life is the most fragile God has created. No human can live forever. Today or tomorrow you will die. No matter who you are, how rich, strong or smart you are, you will die. As a leader can you wonder how your people will remember you? What is your legacy? What have you done as a leader to make your people happy, united, proud and dignified? As a leader, you must ask yourself that question: what will happen to my country and my family after my death if there is no structure for long-term stability, and a peaceful and democratic take-over of power? Imagine after your death – with the help of a powerful European country – one of your enemies or opposite political leaders became president and there was no one who could stop him/her to do whatever he/she wanted to your country or take revenge on your family: borrowing large amounts of money in the name of your country for his/her own use and that money will be paid back with a huge interest rate by the citizens' tax of the country for the next 200 years or more. Assassination of people based on religion or ethnicity, specially those who used to work with the former government, imprisonment of political leaders, their followers and their family without judgment. All the money stolen by the previous president and his government will be transferred into the new president's personal bank account, including the sales of any cars, any houses, and any shares in any companies owned by the previous president and his government. You can corrupt most of the army officers, you can corrupt most of the political leaders, but you cannot corrupt all the people who are the guardians of peace, stability, and progress for many generations of the nation.

You must do whatever it takes to keep your country away from predators. To achieve that, you need good structure, good laws based on your culture and tradition. Trained good men and women who will carry on the fight for democracy, stability and progress (politically, economically and socially) and peace. Above all, laws and structure that do not allow any president to behave like a God. We do not want a president who can decide alone the future of his country. We do not want a president who can change alone the constitution of the country he governs in order to stay in power for longer than what the constitution of the country allows (a maximum of two terms is enough). When you are in power, the army officers and all the security personnel pretend they will back you up anytime for fear of losing their jobs, even their life. Your people pretend they love you unconditionally because they fear if they do not show you love, you can order the army to hurt them.

Western countries have the quality of life the people enjoy now, the stability and peace of life, because of the sacrifices made by their great-grandparents during the First and Second World War. Specially during the Second World War, people in the Western countries fought a bloody battle to protect the unity and integrity of their countries against the might of the German army. Millions of lives were lost. Starvation and diseases killed many millions more people. After that, the Western politicians learnt from the past mistakes and built structure, created laws to maintain peace and stability.

<u>**Structure**</u>: A constitution that brings everyone together, no one is ignored, forgotten or voiceless (Muslim, Christian and other religious groups are together). Anyone's view is taken into account. Rich people and poor people are all equal in the eyes of the law. You will be judged according to the crime you have committed and not judged by how much money you have or who you know or the type of job you do.

<u>**Create laws**</u>: No one is guilty until proven by the court of law. No one will be sent to jail based on rumours or fake news. The country is very organised. You know your right and have the right to fight to get justice. You also know your limit (what to say or do and what not to say or do). When you cross the line, you will be punished. Western laws do not care who you are, who you know; the law does not care about your celebrity status and the law is above anyone.

<u>**Western countries are very proud and do not allow or tolerate**</u> any foreign power to interfere in their internal affairs. Anyone, politician or not, caught taking a bribe to do his/her job will be sacked
immediately. No political leader is allowed to change the constitution or the laws for his/her own advantages. All leaders have a legitimate right to care, protect and save his/her citizens. When any citizen is in difficulty abroad, the Western government must do whatever is needed – to care, to assist their citizen in that foreign country and must do whatever it takes to make sure their citizen can return home safely. If anything happens to their citizen (in the worse scenario, like rape or death) anyone responsible for that crime will brought to justice.

<u>**Maintained peace**</u>: Western countries build a strong army to protect their motherland. Each country selects the best men and woman to do the job. These men and woman are well-trained, well-educated and well-prepared, well motivated to do whatever it takes to protect the integrity, unity and peace of their respective countries. These men and women are prepared to die for their respective countries rather than risking the peace and stability of the country by taking bribes. It is impossible to try and bribe any security officer because you will be caught. What can one or two people do, when thousands and thousands of officers are working around the clock to identify and neutralise the enemies and the traitors. Everyone and anyone is under surveillance in case one or two get distracted and weaken to take bribes – after all, we are all human, and human beings have their weakness, that is the reason everyone is under surveillance. From top to bottom you are being watched and you do not know who is watching who; it is a web because without security nothing is possible to be achieved. When you are in the armed forces in Western countries, you do not know who is watching who.

The Western politicians taught the people and themselves to respect their rules and law. One of the most important rules is anyone must respect the result of the vote of the people to avoid any division. It is forbidden to any leader to use force and intimidation to rule. The need of the people must be your number one priority; and what people need is peace, stability and education for everyone, freedom of speech and religion, equal opportunities for everyone, jobs, good healthcare for everyone, and justice.

You could be a great leader, a charismatic leader who wants the best for his people. Life is very fragile and short; do you wonder what will happen to your country and your people after your death? Without any long-term structure for stability, peace and democracy no matter what you did, your legacy will be destroyed – your family, children, brothers and these who worked with you or for you, their family will be hunted down like common criminals. Look what the West did to Gaddafi and his beautiful country. Libya used to be a paradise compared to the rest of the African countries. Look how his children have been humiliated and killed like dogs. Is this the kind of future you want for your country and your family?

You do not need to be in power to lead your country.

The strength and power of the West is not in their military might, it not their financial muscle or their unity against their common enemies or adversaries but in their patience. Western politicians are extremely patient and if they have to wait many years, they will wait many years for an opportunity to arrive. Once the opportunity is in their hands, they will take it. No matter how big or small the enemy is, they will squash every drop of oxygen from the enemy's lungs until the enemies drop dead.

Education opened my eyes, my thoughts and the way I see the world.

Education allows me to ask questions to myself and also to people who are around me. I just want to know how a continent like Africa and its people were under the control of the West for so long and nothing was done to free African people mentally, economically and physically? The more I go into my research, the more I understand. I came to England to further my education, and everything that was obscured in my mind started making sense.

How the West kept an absolute control over African countries.

There are four things I identified: the structure left behind after African countries' independence; the extreme poverty;

psychology war; and the use of the divide and conquer policy.

The structure left to control African countries after their independence is:

The colonizers (Western countries)

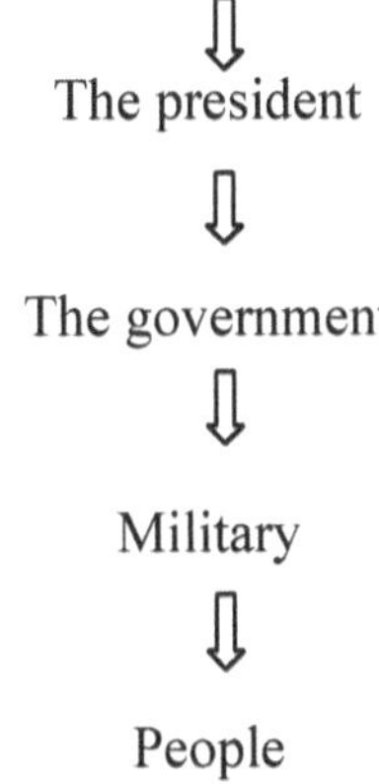

The president

The government

Military

People

The colonizers (Western countries)

The colonizers came as traders; discovered the immense natural resources which are vital for their emergent industrial countries and made the autochthone slave by force. African traditions and culture were destroyed; their natural resources were ripped off. The new nations were born. You can have the same ethnics group in two or three different countries.

To control African leaders, the colonizers (Western countries), before they left Africa, **chose** the most loyal and most unpopular as president. If the chosen one has to keep his job, he must do whatever the colonizers tell him to do. To avoid any surprise, the chosen president's most trusted advisers must be under the supervision of the colonizer's lieutenants. The key ministerial posts like defence, communication, finance, justice, foreign affairs, and transport are under the eye of the colonizer's secret services called advisers. These advisers have access to the president's palace 24/7.

With that system in place, the colonizers are free to have all the natural resources of the country they control.

The colonizers make African people believe democracy (their democracy) is the only way to abolish poverty, to have stability, peace and progress. Where there is democracy, there is always division, instability. The nation must be very strong, experienced and well-organised to survive such periods. African countries are not strong and not organised, therefore instability and division will drag African countries to war; tribes against tribes, Muslims against Muslims, Christians against Christians or Muslims against Christians. Many innocent lives will always be lost during presidential campaigns.

By introducing the system of election, the colonizers make African people believe they have the power to choose their leaders. Election is just a delusion. In any election we have opposition and where there is opposition, there is always division. There are no clean and fair elections in Africa. The head of state is already chosen the year before the date of the election by the colonizer.

I'm a believer and as a Christian believe in God; and the colonizers are not God and sometimes their strategy, the machine oppressor of the colonizer goes wrong in their colonies. When it happens, someone they do not expect to be president becomes president. After years of misery, a good leader comes to power. A leader who is prepared to challenge the way things are organised, someone who is prepared to challenge the system in place – a system that does not care about the well-being of the African people but cares more about the colonizers and their interests. For the colonizers, that leader needs to be neutralised, killed before his people wake up. To achieve their goal the system they created will be used and the good leader is killed either by:

- Poisoning (slow and painful death).
- Car crash or plane crash .
- Bullet in his head by his own security officers .

If none of these steps mentioned above can not kill a good African leader because he is loved by his people then the colonizers create a rebellion. Rebels are recruited from a different religion or different ethnic group to the president that the West wanted to remove from power. These rebels are brainwashed, well-armed, well-trained, well-equipped military and under the supervision of western special forces attack the good leader elected by the people. Rebellion always works in any African country because most African countries armed forces are under-trained, under-paid, under-motivated, under-equipped, and very corrupt from top to bottom. The leader, including his government and closest collaborators, will be made to leave by force and become a refugee in a neighbouring African country. A rebel's goal is to humiliate or massacre the president, his wife, and all his children as well as his minister's family. This is how Western power sent a message to other African leaders. To tell these African leaders, if they do not do what they are being told to do, they will face the same fate. And sometimes when lucky if they (president, his government and their family) are captured, they will be sent to prison for life for defending their countries and the president will be replaced by the most corrupt leader. A suitable Leader is chosen by the west to protect their interest. A leader who is prepared to make his own people sweat blood to make the west richer.

The traitors – these African intellectuals who pretend by day to defend the country, its people and its interest and by night receive instructions from the colonizer to spy on the government they work for to provide all the information: the military strength and weakness, the decision taken by the government to stop the colonizer to overpower military and politically the legal government of African countries, – The traitor spy on the people the good leader trusts the most. In this way they can be corrupted to work for the colonizer and if the leader's trusted companions refuse the proposal of the colonizer (worked for the colonizer instead of the good leader) then the colonizer can use force by threatening their family). Any information's needed to make the colonizer's job easy when the time come to overthrow any unsuitable leader to the west interest in Africa is welcome.

Traitors

After our so-called independence, African countries lacked the elite or intellectuals to reorganise their respective countries in Africa. Some people were selected by the colonizers to study in European countries to help their respective countries in Africa. At the time, African people refused to send their children to Europe after witnessing what the colonizers did to them in their own countries. For these African parents, sending your child to Europe is like sending your loved one to prison or to be a slave again to the colonizers, and no one was prepared to make that sacrifice. So the colonizer took full advantage of the situation and selected people who the colonizer thought were loyal and could be trusted.

After years of study and training, African new intellectuals went to their respective countries in Africa to organise their countries under the supervision of the colonizers. African people stupidly thought these elite people were their saviours. They put their trust in the hands of these intellectuals, these elites, to propel and develop their respective countries. But the colonizers had other ideas. The colonizers left Africa physically but were still present, still had an eye through these elites, these intellectuals, on what was going on in Africa. Most of these elites or intellectuals were recruited to work for the colonizers instead of working for their respective countries.

When these elites or intellectuals finished their studying, they went back to their respective countries. The colonizers used their influence, connections, and sometimes used force and intimidation to introduce these African elites or intellectuals in every part of the administration of their respective countries. Because these intellectuals or elites had the best education and the best training, they occupied the top jobs in every administration of their respective countries.

We can find these elites or intellectuals in the:
- Army and any other security system
- Finance system
- Justice system
- Communication system
- Foreign affairs
- Immigration
- Education
- Health system
- Churches: priests, pastors and higher posts in the churches
- Mosques: Imams and higher ranks in the mosques
- Political leaders
- Businessmen and businesswomen

The same old system is still in place in this 21st century in Africa. That is the reason why there are so many wars in

Africa – because the new generation wants more than what their parents have. They want good education, good healthcare, good roads, good infrastructure, good jobs where they can afford to have enough money to pay the bills, to afford to send their children to school – and to have a decent life. To achieve all these things, to satisfy the need of the new generation, any government needs money. Money that is not available because the colonizers prioritise the needs of their respective countries. The colonizers take everything that IS needed to build their countries and give some to the African governments who do not care about the people, and as long as that government has the backing of the West no one can remove it from power. When life is hell for African people, their corrupt government and their closest allies live a good life.

For the sake of the stability and progress of African countries, these traitors must be identified and neutralised as soon as possible. These traitors are a cancer in African society. They cause the worst damage because they are among us, they know our culture, our tradition, they live with us day in day out, they know our weakness and all the problems African people have in society (division issues, religion issues, tribal issues and tribal alliance). African traitors inform the colonizer who uses the information on all these problems and issues to maximise their control on African countries, the African government.

President

Election is based on the rule of law. In a democratic country, all political parties have access to the media and all political parties are given the same chance to win. It is fair and square, no cheating.

In Africa, election is based on corruption, manipulation, fake news, intimidation, bribes. The party in power always wins, no matter what, unless there is a military coup or the current president is assassinated. Presidential candidates use religion and ethnics issue as a programme to govern, which creates more division among the population. African people do not support a political leader because of his ideology, his projects for the nation, but support a political leader based on their belonging of religion and ethnicity with that political leader. That is another issue that creates more division to African people.

Most presidents come to power through a military coup. A military coup is when a group of army officers decide to remove by force a current president and replace him by another corrupt leader in the name of democracy. No military coup can take place without the approval of a Western power. When a military coup has happened without the approval of a Western power, another military coup takes place to remove the new leaders. When a military coup happens, there are always many civilian deaths.

A military coup is a warning to African leaders. It is a way the Western power tells African leaders that they can be removed anytime if the West wants that, therefore they must follow orders if they want to keep their jobs. For these governments, if they do not do what they have been told to do, it's *au revoir*.

The president is like a living god; he has an absolute power about everything in the country. All decisions regarding the country must go through him. Only the president can accept or refuse any decision that does not suit him. He can do whatever he wants: the public fund can be used for his own need; any minister can be removed as he pleases; he can borrow enormous amounts of money using the name of the country and keep most of that money in his own bank account in foreign countries (Europe).

The ministers who are supposed to guide the president to make good decisions for the country will not dare tell the president that the decisions are not good for the country, if they want to keep their jobs. Power can change hands at any time. Any government that has no interest to care for its people can be removed anytime. The president knows that and his government knows that. Therefore, the president, his government and other people linked to his power, must steal as much as possible in case someone else is chosen by the colonizers to replace the president in power. The stolen money is kept outside the country and most of the time in European banks. These ministers are there to say yes to everything that the president and his advisors decide. These ministers are more concerned about how much money they will make through corruption than thinking about the future of the country. These ministers are more concerned about the privileges and the power their post gave them, than worrying about the extreme poverty and the misery of their people.

The president is above the constitution. He can change the law at any time as he pleases and no one can stop him. The president controls the army by giving the strategic post to his family members and friends. Under the eye and observation of the Western countries these presidents are the best leaders in Africa. When these leaders come to Europe, the are received by Western leaders with all the honour and respect a good leader deserves. For Western leaders, the lives of African people is not important. Many African people can starve to death, many African people can be killed by their own government forces – it's OK as long as these African leaders provide what Western countries need to build and strengthen their economies and prestige. The day a European journalist exposes these African leaders about their cruelty against their own people, it's only at that moment the European leaders will put pressure (economically and military) on these leaders to behave in a democratic manner (allow freedom of speech) for a short period of time or they will be removed.

Army

African countries do not have an army. They have men and women in uniform that are paid to protect a corrupt president, a corrupt government; they are badly paid and use their uniform to collect bribes from a population that is struggling already to make ends meet. Anyone, and in particular motorists, who refuse to pay the amount of money requested is humiliated and can have his driving licence confiscated until he pays the amount of money requested. If the motorist does not have the money asked, he will have to come later to the police station to get his licence back.

An African army is not fit to be called an ARMY. An army that is not capable to protect the whole country if there is any attack from terrorists or any rebellion from a neighbouring African country, is not an army. The African army is made only to bully and intimidate the population. The African army is made specially to be used against its own defenceless people. Army officers call themselves brave, strong and ready to die, only if it's to oppress the population who have no use of any weapon.

Army officers have a licence to kill, to intimidate, to rape, to torture, to imprison anyone who has verbally abused the president or challenged his authority. Any civilian who opposes or criticises the government is punished. Any opposition leader who challenges the president is crushed.

What can we do? There two things we can do.

1- Education

From nursery to university, African people must be taught how to be honest, proud and respectful. African people must learn how to love their respective countries and work together as one to protect their countries when their motherland is under attack by terrorists, rebels or any other enemies. African people need to know the meaning of the word *integrity* and apply it in their life. African people need to be taught how to respect their laws. The African people need to know anyone who attacks their countries, no matter their religion or ethnics is their enemy (it could be your dad, your mum, your brothers, your sisters, your cousins, nephews, your nieces, your friends). And that enemy must be punished, neutralised by any means. We must teach our people how to protect their neighbour, the same way they need to be protected.

I had lived in the Ivory Coast before coming to Europe. Back then if your house was in flames, your neighbour rushed to your rescue to extinguish the flames. You are not left alone.

The colonizers always used your neighbour to conquer the land they envied. If you quarrel, fight or have a bad relationship with your neighbour he will not help you in your period of need. In fact, if your house is burning, your neighbour will put petrol on the fire so that the fire will cause more damage to your property. By creating a good relationship with your neighbour, it will be difficult for the colonizers to attack your land and your people.

Our elites, intellectuals, must be educated in their countries of origin, in Africa. African people need to modernise and reorganise the education system to allow their students to achieve their goal. African people must provide all the equipment, the help the student needs to progress. African people do not need any education system which is too expensive, disorganised and penalises the bright and poor student and favours the bad and rich students of the country. The books use in African schools or universities must be produce in African by African authors.

2-   The Balance of Power.

Some African leaders (very few) come to power with very good intentions for their countries. They want peace, unity, stability. These leaders want to create jobs and raise the living standard of their people. But the colonizers, through the system in place, put so much pressure on the new leaders to favour their interest against the well-being of their own people.

These leaders or presidents have a choice to make, a dilemma. They either serve the colonizer and sacrifice or leave their people in extreme poverty – by doing that these leaders can live peacefully with their wife and children – or they serve their people, by doing so these leaders go against the colonizers who will do whatever it takes not to lose the control of the country and their interest.

African leaders or presidents are human beings like any other human being. They are not God. They want to live as long as possible. They want to watch their children grow up and be successful. They want to be remembered for the work they have done for their country. They want to be honoured and respected. Who can blame them? These African leaders or presidents know the colonizers have the power (military, economically, politically) to do whatever they want in any African country. Having these thoughts makes good African leaders or presidents start panicking; they start wondering who can protect their lives, their family, children and their people?

People must find ways to protect their good leaders from the wrath of the colonizers. When an African leader has to make a choice between the wrath of the people and the wrath of the colonizers, without any hesitation that leader must choose the people over the colonizers. The leader must fear the wrath of the people more than the wrath of the colonizers. This is the only way African people can get their freedom. African people need to be united as one. African people must put aside their religions and ethnics differences for the survival, stability and progress of their nations. African people must be prepared to make the ultimate sacrifices to defend the leader who is prepared to defend the natural resources and the independence of his country and his people. It does not matter if the good leader is from the north, the south, the east, the west, the centre of the country, Muslim or Christian. What matters is what that leader is going to do to make your life better: be able to pay for your medicine bill, your water and electricity bill, to have a roof over your head, to have job to live a decent life, to be protected by the law. To have a voice in your own country. To be respect and care for when needed.

Poverty

Having been born and bred in the Ivory Coast (west Africa), and grown up in my country of origin, I cannot figure out how Western countries kept African countries under their control for so long. From the period of slavery, through African so-called independence to now in this 21st century, Western power still controls African countries, African government and African natural resources with an iron fist. Through my adult life I had the desire, the appetite and curiosity to understand the mechanism of the Western supremacy over African countries. Through my study and research, I found out how African people and their government were dominated by Western countries for so long and finally I found out how. The key word is extreme poverty. Extreme poverty comes with greed, division, xenophobia, Islamophobia, mental inferiority, instability, war, violence, increased crime and vices. Extreme poverty allows Western power to go through African government like blood goes through the human body; Western power knows African weakness and strength and they have used our weakness to gain whatever they need. Poverty is not just the inability to feed your people or pay your bills. Poverty is a mental state. Imagine, just imagine, the African and the European people switch countries. The African people took over European countries with the institution, all the infrastructure, knowing everything is ready to run; the European people took over African countries where everything needs to be built – the hospitals, the roads, the colleges / universities, the rail stations, the telecommunication system. What will happen after fifteen or twenty years?

Poverty is one of the most efficient weapons used by the Western countries to keep African countries divided, therefore easy to manipulate and control. Ninety percent of the population is struggling daily to put food on the table, to pay its monthly water bill, electricity bill and send its children to school.

Poverty has stopped the most talented individuals to flourish, to show to the world what he/she can do. Poverty affects your mind: the way you think, the way you behave, the way you see things. A poor person hopes to have food every day, a job that will allow him/her to pay for electricity, water bills monthly, to send his/her children to school and to be able to afford hospital bills in case someone is sick. Things we Africans who live in Europe have. It does not mean there is no poverty in the African community in Europe. To allow their population to live with pride and dignity, Western governments created a social service to look after the disabled and the unemployed so their people will not be forced to beg for food or be humiliated, be abused, or be exploited by parents or relatives. The social service in Europe allows the disabled and unemployed people to have a roof over their head; they have medicine free if there are sick; and money monthly or weekly for food and clothes, and to pay for the gas and electricity bills. The social service allows Western people to be independent and responsible for their own life until they have a job.

Take away the social service in one of the most powerful countries in Europe. Countries like Germany, the United Kingdom or France. Without social service, those countries will collapse as badly as African countries. People in these countries will live in extreme poverty which will feed extreme corruption. Extreme corruption that will bring a chaotic system, insecurity, division, instability, increased vices and war. Social service is a foundation of stability, peace and progress. The social service allows citizens to have normal living conditions.

The social service is in place in Western countries because they have stability, they are organised, they have a very good system in place: law and order, a good justice system, a good police force who do a very good job to protect and serve the people, and every company (big or small) must pay their taxes. Each employee pays their taxes. It is illegal to pay your employees in cash. Any company or employer who breaks the rules is punished heavily. To keep the social service, Western government created more jobs for their citizens. The more citizens work, more money goes to the government's safe.

Hospitals: In each hospital we have doctors, midwives, nurses, associate physicians, laboratories (biochemistry, haematology, virology, cytology, microbiology, histology). Each laboratory can create jobs for 15–25 people. We have consultants, electricians, porters, ambulance services; we have people who work in the kitchen from chefs to cleaners, we have cleaners who look after the floor and toilets of the hospitals and many more. Each hospital can employ ten to twenty thousand people.

Public transport: People need to move around to work. The transport must be easy to access no matter where you are. Transport is vital for the development of the country.

In the UK we have the Underground, trains and trams system that allows anyone to move easily from north to south and from east to west. Buses are 7 days a week and some busy areas are bused 24 hours a day.

We Africans can copy from the West to create as many jobs as we can for our population – telecommunication systems, supermarkets, banks and many more jobs.

We have three major types of poverty in Africa. Intellectual, security and alimentary poverty:

Intellectual Poverty:

Study is the most efficient route in Africa to get out of poverty. African parents invest everything they have; they sacrifice so much to allow their children to be educated. At the end of their study, after all the struggle, these students expect to have a job so that as a son or daughter, you can look after your parents or at least pay back the money your parents used to finance your study. Unfortunately, there are no jobs available to do. If you are lucky enough to know someone in a higher place, you have to pay or bribe that person for a job. Almost all students who graduated from university stay unemployed, when African countries desperately need doctors, nurses, scientists, pharmacists, consultants, engineers and many more to propel African countries. African universities produce very good students who need the opportunity to show their intelligence, to show what they can do. All these brainy students are left to waste. There is no structure to help train these students to help their country. The only solution that remains is to leave your country in Africa and try to enter (legally or illegally) any European country and try to rebuild a new life.

Our so-called leaders, when they are sick or one of their family members is sick, they do not hesitate to fly to Europe to use the facilities of European health services.

Alimentary Poverty:
The Ivory Coast, where I come from, is the number one producer of cocoa and number third producer of coffee in the world in 1994.

The most fertile land in my country is used to grow these two main products. When I was growing up in the Ivory Coast I was shocked and did not understand why the government had encouraged the Ivorian to produced so much cocoa and coffee, when most Ivorians eat a lot of rice, banana plantain, cassava, gnam and meat and fish. Why not use our fertile land to grow what we eat most? We as a nation must be able to feed our nation first. We as a nation we must be able to satisfy our domestic consummation in food. What I find strange above all, is that my country is the first producer in the world of cocoa and third in coffee, but Ivorians cannot afford to buy chocolate or have coffee during their breakfast because these products are too expensive to buy. There is no logic and we can not blame Western countries for that. Our leaders 'forced' African farmers to produce products that satisfy Western people's appetites, ultimately starving their own African people.

Poverty Securitaire:
The army is poorly equipped, poorly maintained and men and women in these jobs are poorly paid. The morale of men and women who have the responsibility to protect the country is very low. Any leader who comes to power, instead of choosing men and women who have the ability, the experience to secure the country, choose people from his/her religious or ethnic group. Most of the time these people lack the professionalism required to do these important jobs. That is why we have mutiny in the African army. For a yes or no, these soldiers use their weapons and bring the country to its knees if their demand (an increase in their wages, and better living conditions) is not satisfied. Without any proper and professional army, how do you

expect to protect the country against our predators, who envy our natural resources so badly?

Anyone who controls the aerial space controls the security of a country. Because African countries do not have the technology to protect their aerial space. Any European country can spy on them. Any European army can violate the aerial space of any African country. Any government who cannot protect its country exposes his country and its people to any danger like a coup or civilian war. Our so-called leaders do not care about the security of their countries. They recruited people from their tribe, trained them well in Europe, gave them the best and modern military equipment money can buy, not to protect the country but protect their weak and corruptible government. When Western governments are fed up and tired of these weak and corruptible African governments they can be replaced by another weak and corruptible government. When a new government takes office in a powerful Western country, it all depends on the ideology – it could be a democrat, a socialist, a republican or liberal leader. The new Western leader just replaces the old weak and corruptible African government with another weak and corruptible government.

Nothing will change, the old African leaders are replaced by others, not because the new Western government wants democracy but the Western government want its own chosen people to deal with because the old African leaders are just too close to the former government replaced in Western countries.

Psychology war.

Most nations on the planet were colonised and have tasted the humiliation of being colonised. But no colonised nations went through what African countries have witnessed. When the colonizer came and discovered all the

African natural resources, natural resources that were vital for the survival of their country's prestige and economy strength, the colonizer wanted it all by any means. To achieve that, the colonizer needed to make African people believe everything that came from Africa was bad, and everything that comes from Western countries was good. Grown-up and being told every day at school you are a slave and Europeans are your masters, you end up believing you are not good. You believe as an African that you were a slave because your colonizer is smarter, more intelligent, stronger than you. Intellectually, as an African you feel inferior to any Western person. Our colonizer told us: Black means bad, distasting, ugly; and White means beautiful, pure and good. Through my childhood and my adulthood, I have tried to understand these ideologies put to us, as a young African man grown up in Africa. I have never understood why when someone died in your family you must dress in black from head to toe for the funeral, and when there is a new-born baby you must dress in white? Where that regulation comes from I never asked and I never understood these practices. To be free physically, you need to be free mentally and psychologically. When your mind is not free you are trapped and as a human being you become a slave forever; your children, grandchildren and future generations are trapped in the same way, mentally. Western countries created some words to justify why black is bad and white is good. In Western culture and languages we have terms like black Friday, black book and white noise.

Black Friday: Black Friday is the name given to the shopping day after Thanksgiving (USA). That day so many people go out to shop that it causes traffic accidents and sometimes violence.

Black book: A black book is a book that contains a list of secret contacts or the names of people liable to be punished.

White noise: White noise is a random signal having equal intensity at different frequencies, giving it a constant power spectral density. The term white noise is used in many scientific and technical discipline like physics, acoustic engineering, telecommunication and statistical forecasting.

African countries were portrayed as shit countries with no future.

As an African man in a foreign country, when you are sat in front of the TV and constantly watching negative images of your continent, you are not happy. You constantly watch a young child covered in dust and walking mile after mile on a dusty road without choosing to collect water, water shared by animals to take home to be used as drinking water. You constantly see news about Africa where people are dying in their thousands because their own government cannot feed them and rely on Western generosity for food.

A black child growing up and watching these images will be brainwashed. That child will believe these stories and will find it very difficult one day to travel to his parents' country of origin in Africa. For a white boy who has never visited any African country, these negative images will feed his belief about the supremacy of his race to the black race. Africa is a big continent made of 52 countries. When something happens in one country in Africa, a finger is pointed at the whole continent, but it is not only about war, extreme poverty, killing, dissipating people like meat. In any country in the world there are always good sights and bad sights. In any country you can find beautiful places, and places of duty – the same goes for European countries.

How do you expect your colleagues at work to respect you when all the images about your continent are always negative? The more I live in England and travel around in other Europeans countries I can see for myself – even if European countries are all organised, all healthy, all stable and European citizen respect more their laws – they have their own problems. European countries also have poor people who struggle to feed their children. There are also European people who live in houses that lack electricity and running water. There are beggars in the street or on the trains. Women sell their bodies to get some cash to pay for food, alcohol or clothes. Even if the conditions of poor Europeans are not as bad as for poor Africans, they are still poor people.

Grown up in the Ivory Coast I did not know European countries had poor people until I started travelling around European countries. All the TV channels in the Ivory Coast always show positive images about European countries, so I'm confused and do not understand why, while European channels are showing negative images about Africa, African channels always show positive images about European countries. So that black people born in any European country try so hard to differentiate themselves to African people.

I was a child when my best friend's aunt told one of his cousins that he was so dark he made her want to vomit. I was shocked and did not understand why someone's dark skin colour would make someone else want to throw up. Then I grew up and observed that there are some parts of Black countries, whether in Africa or the Caribbean, where a lighter skin colour is regarded as God's gift of beauty; while being black is ugly, disgusting, and unacceptable. Some people are so ashamed of their black skin colour that they bleach their skin to make it light. Those who have light skin, bleach it to look even lighter. These who keep their black colour want to make sure their children are not as black as them; therefore, they are willing to do whatever it takes to have mixed-race children. The lighter you are, the more successful you become in life. We are black because we have in abundance a substance in our skin called melanin. The more melanin you have, the darker the colour of your skin; the less you have of that substance, the lighter your skin colour. No one choose his/her skin colour. It's genetic. No one can control what type of skin colour you will get. Love yourself no matter the type of skin you are in.

Being black African

Being black African in this world is hard, it is like a curse. Black Africans are the most oppressed and humiliated on the planet. Instead of working together to help each other to be prosperous, successful and united, we hate each other. The worst crimes committed on black Africans are by black African people. Why black Africans hate each other is beyond me. Is it poverty? Is it stupidity? Is it ignorance or just madness? Seeing someone in your community being successful, being in a stable relationship with his wife will make that person the enemy number one of the community. The same community will try, and will do whatever it takes to break the relationship to pieces, then laugh at you when you are going through hell.

We Africans want to be free, at the same time we do not want to fight to get our freedom. African people want to be united and strong but they tear each other up when the opportunity arrives. Any country who attacks either UK, France or Italy will be ganged by all European countries. In Africa, if any country is attacked, others African countries will join forces with the attacker to bring the country who was attacked to its knees. We Africans, if we want to be respected, we must behave as respectable people. Blaming Western countries is a cheap excuse to our leader for being irresponsible, ignorant and powerless to provide to their people the stability and progress needed to be a successful nation. Western countries are not all responsible for what happens to us either in Africa or Europe.

Black African in Europe

For culture reasons, most Africans decide to have a wife who is from their country of origin. Why? Because I believe these men want to eat the same African food and share their culture and language when their children arrive. It is not cheap to bring someone from Africa to Europe legally. You must provide your bank statement to prove that you can look after your wife financially when she arrives. You must have a job and a place big enough for two people. It is not easy to fulfil these conditions. Once your wife arrives, you start having children. Then she finds out from friends or relatives that women have power over men, the same power men have over women in Africa: A woman can get her husband out of the house based on false accusations – like her man has beaten her up or he raped her. When the police arrive, they (police) will ask the man to leave because women are more vulnerable than men to survive in the street.

Two examples:

Example 1
A friend I knew for a long time brought his wife from his country of origin (east Africa) to England. They started to have children (two boys and girl). They had a pretty decent living standard because both were doing a good job. Their life was good so they started to get a mortgage together. Life was perfect, then his dad got sick so he needed to go back home to Africa (east Africa). Thank God, his dad's health got better and he decided to rejoint his family in Europe (England). He was already at the airport when his wife called him and told him the house they shared with their three children was sold and there was no point in him coming home because she had moved out with the children.

How cruel somebody can be? After all these years together she jeopardised the family's future for her own greed. What can you do? Mentally, if you are not strong, anyone might commit suicide.

Example 2

A close friend of a friend from west Africa came to England illegally. To make a living he was working with fake documents. Then he met a black British woman who came from the same country as him (west Africa). They started dating and had a child together. After two years she decided she did not need him anymore to raise their child. She knew the immigration state of her man. She knew how he got the job and where he was working. So she came out with an evil plan to get rid of the man. The man was at work when the woman called an immigration officer, telling them where her man was working, how he got the job and the documents he was using to work. She told the immigration officers everything they needed to know – like what he looked like, the type of clothes he wore and his birthmark, including the name he used and the location of the job. With all this information, the immigration officer went to the address given, picked the man up and put him in prison until all the paperwork was ready to send him back to his country of origin. While in prison he tried to contact his wife so that she could get a solicitor to get him out, but all the time her phone was off so he called his close friend. The close friend then contacted the community who raised emergency funds to get a solicitor who fought very hard to get the man released because he had a young child. When released he found out the woman with whom he had a child, was the one who back-stabbed him – so he could not go back to her because he did not know what else she was capable of after what she did to him.

Those are just two examples among countless others. How many more African lives are being destroyed by

African people? Those two examples show how much hate, betrayal and hurt we Africans are causing each other.

How can you do that to someone else's child?

How can you live your life peacefully when you destroy someone else's life in Europe, knowing the sacrifices his parents had to make to send that child to Europe? You also know how much hope our parents put on us Africans who came to Europe.

Children who are involved in these situations have seen their lives been affected. It affects their study, their ability to have a normal life. These kids grow up and leave school at a very young age. To make a living they often get involved in crime, become drug dealers, thieves and gang members. They become addicted to drugs and fear no one.

England is a multicultural country. We have Pakistanis, Indian, Chinese, Nepalese etc., children of many nationalities, but why is it always African children who are being killed in the street for gang-related crime while Asian kids are more educated? Asian kids become doctors, pharmacists, scientists, consultants, engineers, but black kids are either in jail or in the morgue. We as parents cannot blame the system or Western governments of racism. When things go wrong it is always someone's fault, this is why we are not going anywhere. It is a pity watching talented African kids be killed every week in the streets of the UK, especially in London, for gang-related issues. These African kids are as good as any other kids. African parents need to grow up and put the future of their children before their own selfish interests. When your child becomes a doctor, pharmacist, scientist etc., after all the sacrifices you have made, it is a blessing. You can die peacefully knowing you have done what a good parent needed to do to give to your child a life.

India and Pakistan have nuclear weaponry. Their scientists built their own nuclear bomb without the help of any European scientists. Most of Pakistan and India scientists studied in Europe. They used their knowledge to help their respective countries. We Africans can do that, we can build our own infrastructure with the help of our children who were born in Europe.

Black African in Africa.

In Africa you need to work to be able to feed your family. The social service does not exist, but those who have food share with those who have nothing. Families are looking after each other and share the little that they have. There is solidarity, but not as good as in European countries.

There are no benefits for those unemployed or disabled, like in Europe. There are few jobs and most of these jobs are occupied by men. It is not an excuse for women to sit there and expect their husband to pay the entire bill. As a man in Africa, when you are working you must look after your brothers, sisters, cousins and your in-laws etc., as much as you can. Money is therefore tied up.

Any woman who lets only her husband pay the rent/mortgage, the electricity bill, and food bill, becomes the man's slave. For your own respect, your own dignity and prestige, for the woman's well-being, a woman must participate and share all the expenses in the house. There are jobs she can do, such as selling vegetables, fruits, and clothes at the market to bring in some money. The little bit of money can be useful in case there are any emergencies such as: someone dies in the husband's family or the woman's family, kids have an accident and urgently need money for medical costs, or school fees for the kids etc. Women who participate and share the bills with their husband are more secure and more respected in their relationship.

Laziness is not acceptable and it is the reason men in Africa cheat on the woman.

Grown up, when you are in a relationship, that relationship is based more on 'I need you' than 'I love you'.

The real love is when you are a teenager about 16–18 years old. You live with you parents, you have no bills to pay, you do not have to worry about food or hospital bills and you meet your girlfriend who is the same age as you and also who is living with her parents where she does not have any bills to pay like you. I call that real love. You do not need her and she does not need you. You two are together to have fun. No worries to think about.

When you grow up and have children to feed, when you have bills to pay. When you have children's future to think about, you get together with a woman not mainly because of love but it's more of need than love. A man cannot marry a woman because she is pretty, she knows how to dress well or she has a good style. You get married because you need someone to help share the price of your bills so that you can save some money, and you can improve your living conditions. Having a woman in your bed is a plus, like a cherry on a cake. If African women do not understand the reality in a relationship and expect their man to pay for all the expenses, do not be surprise if that man cheats on you or dumps you for another woman.

Working together brings stability and progress. Children can get what they need: food is available, school fees are paid, the school uniform is provided so teachers do not need to send children back home. Children living in those condition can flourish and can achieve some very good results and participate in the development, progress of their country where their parents came from.

Message to all Africans

African people must stop dreaming about a divine force that one day will come and free them or stop them suffering. African people must not expect the West or any foreign power to free them. African natural resources are the envy of all the world and the super powers of the world want it badly, for free. The only way the super powers can grab these natural resources for free is to use African weakness against Africans. Africans have two major weakness: Ethnic division (one ethnic group against another) and religious difference (Muslim against Christian, Christian against Muslim or Muslim against Muslim).

Ethnic group

The independence of African countries was given by the West. The first president was chosen by the West from the ethnic group; the West thinks that the people of that ethnic group are more loyal to them and therefore those people can safeguard their interest in that country. The first president from the ethnic group strongly believed it is their birth right to lead the country for ever and no other ethnic group can have the ability to be president. The first president used that opportunity that was given by the West to place his people in the best jobs at any level of the administration – especially in the army and secret service – in case any other ethnic group tries to be president and that person could be removed by force.

After twenty to thirty years under the leadership of the same ethnic group, there are no changes. The people are young and educated but there are no job opportunities unless you are from the ethnic group of the ruling party then you can have a job, if not you will be unemployed for life irrespective of your quality and intelligence. Students get frustrated, angry and are not prepared to tolerate that injustice anymore. Specially as a student when you are the best of your class and see a student who is at the bottom of the class in terms of grades and that person gets a job before you, just because of his/her ethnic group – it's heart-breaking.

Under the leadership of the same ethnic group, the health care system is a big mess. Poor people are dying in their masses and no one can be punished because it is the same people in charge and when one of them (people who lead the country) is sick they can fly to Europe to be looked after. Under the leader of the same ethnic group the administration is chaotic. You have to bribe people to do their own jobs, the same jobs there are paid monthly. They come to work when they want and leave when they want. Nothing you can do about it. If you need a document urgently you must bribe them. Under the leadership of the same ethnic group the most people who have better living conditions, the better paid jobs, the richest people and people who can make laws to change the life of the population are the same ethnic group in power. No changes can be done without them. They control the country as if the country is their own property. Anyone who controls the economy of any country controls that country.

After years of oppression, intimidation and greed, African people have finally a different political leader who is strong enough, courageous and willing to put his/her life on the line to make changes: improve living conditions, create jobs, stop the West taking our natural resources for free, build schools and universities and share the health of country among the people and, above all, stop the same people who have ruled the country for so long killing the country economically. That political leader is regarded as public enemy number one. If that good political leader becomes president and starts making changes to bring stability, progress, freedom and justice, that leader will be removed by force either by a coup, assassination, a rebellion against the good leader's government or starve his country economically – so that the good leader will not make the changes needed for the progress, stability of the country. With the blessing of the West, who will use their military might and financial muscle to restore the same people who were the first in power after independence, just to carry on sucking the country of its natural resources.

Religious

Muslims and Christians live side by side without any problems in a period of peace. The West colonised Africa and they know very well how to push Muslims against Christians or Christians against Muslims. What the West needed to do was to kill few hundred Muslims or Christians, make up fake history, and with some corrupt imams or pastors and some corrupt political leaders use the fake killing of innocent people as a propaganda to brainwash Muslims or Christians to fight for their survival or the ruling party will kill them all. When someone you trust, someone like an imam or a pastor, is telling news about the killing of Muslims or Christians you will believe it without any evidence. We have a culture of not asking questions, we believe blindly our older, parent or religious leaders. For example, if you are out and see your parent in a street fight, as an African you do not need to ask what is going on, you just get involved in the fight, then after the fight you can ask questions. We African cannot tolerate a political leader who uses a religious difference as a weapon to divide and rule. We cannot tolerate a political leader who uses religion as propaganda.

We need to find a system where Muslims and Christians can live side by side, even in a period of war. We need a system where different ethnic groups can work together and put the interests of the country before their own interests.

Our grandparents were humiliated, abused; and we, the new generation of the 21st century, are also humiliated and abused. We cannot choose our leaders freely. We cannot fix the price of our natural resources; the buyer (the West) fixes the price of our product. If we Africans want our freedom, our peace and better living conditions, we need to fight peacefully. In the near future the Western population will increase; Western political leaders will have more mouths to feed, more people to look after, to care for. The new Western generation will not accept less than what their parents or grandparents have in terms of living conditions. Therefore, Western countries will go out there to find what their economy needs so that they can provide for the new generation and Africa will be the battleground for our natural resources.

BLAME GAME

Do not blame all Western people or their governments for the mess in Africa. Do not hate all the Western population or their government for the chaotic system in Africa.

Western countries do what they have to do to survive.

I have lived in Europe for a long time and I know a lot people who cannot do anything without drinking a cup of coffee in the mornings. In the morning when was going to work and in the evening on my way back home I can see workers queuing to get their cup of coffee. The companies in Western countries have created different types of coffee with different flavours that can suit everyone's tastes.

Chocolate is part of Western people's lives too. Western countries have all types of chocolate. European people love their birth date. They celebrate their birth date anniversary each year at work (bringing chocolate to be share with workmates) and at home with family members buying or baking cakes for the birthday ceremony.). Western people love their cake and love baking. It's part of their culture.

When you do not count the rich in Africa, how many people celebrate their birthday each year - very few.

The mess and chaotic life in Africa is caused by our leaders, with some corrupt minority Western allies. These corrupt minority and very powerful politicians and business men and women are backed by some corrupt politician who used their influence, their connection and financial power to destroy the African state so that they can make more money. Any war against any African country is never about freedom of speech, it's never about democracy or human rights, it's never about stability and peace or saving children and people's lives. War is about money and war is not cheap. These corrupt Westerners will sponsor any African leaders who will be prepared to rape anyone to be in power. Once these African leaders are in power, they must serve these Western allies who sponsor them to be where they are or pay the consequences.

African life is not important, you can kill as much as you can and no one will care because it will not be in the news. Even if it is in the news it will be shown to European people as an African internal affair when in fact it these small, very powerful and very rich Western business people and their politician friends who are responsible; they will always succeed because they know African countries are weak, disorganised, corrupt and divided. They will always be successful to overthrow any government in Africa because they will always have some African politician who has no moral values, who has no conscience whatever, who has no dignity and no pride, who does not care about the future of their country and their population, who does not care about the stability and progress of their country.

Using force to kick Western people from Africa is not the solution. Western countries have more power (financially, military, politically) than African countries. Western countries are more united than African countries. Using force will never work.

I loved my country. I loved my family and I loved my friends but also, I want to live. I wanted to live in a country where I can have an education, get a job and have better living conditions. I wanted to get a wife, have children and watch my kids grow up in a stable environment where they can also have a future. Can I have that kind of life in a foreign country? I really do not know but I have to try.

Finally, I made it to Europe (England) and I was very happy and very excited. I really want to know how Europeans see us Africans and what they thought about us. Growing up in Africa I had that idea that all Westerners are rich, they all have very good well-paid jobs. Westerners all live in big houses, they are all kind, respect other and are not violent people. Now I'm in England, I have the opportunity to verify these old thoughts I used to have about Europeans. I was surprised to see how beautiful and organised England was compared to my country. Domestic waste is kept in a black bag, and collected regularly to keep the streets clean and tidy. Each street, each road, each building has a name. You can move from A to Z very easily as long as you know the address of your destination. The security is so good. There are cameras almost everywhere to protect the population.

Westerners came up with a very good idea that employees are paid per hour and if you do not want to lose money you have to be on time. If you are late you must make up the time lost if you want your full wages. The government is always looking for ways to create more jobs because when more people work, these people pay taxes.

The banks help people who want to go into business by providing money needed to start their companies. Anyone and everyone must pay their taxes; small or big companies pay their taxes. These taxes are used to build hospitals, to build schools/universities, improve roads, invest in research such as cancer, HIV etc. If you want to study, the government will give you all the help needed to study. Any student, any background, no matter who you are (black, white, Asian) can apply for a loan from the government which you will pay back when you start working.

There are so many opportunities; there are so many jobs to choose from. Food and clothes prices are affordable, you can eat anything you want or buy any clothes you want. I was wondering if all European countries were organised that way. My first job was a cleaner in a shopping centre. For a black man without a degree or qualification, you have no choice other than to accept to do this type of work. The job consisted of vacuum cleaning carpets and cleaning the staff toilets. The worst part of that job was to be welcomed every morning by the sight of rotten faeces in a toilet. The employees did not bother to flush the toilets after using them before going home.

Then I moved to being a kitchen porter in a London restaurant. As a kitchen porter, I was astonished by the intensity of the job. It was unbelievably hard, very busy, physically demanding and stressful. Some of the cooking pots used were so large an adult man could fit into them. These jobs were very hard. There were times, during my break time, I would think about going back home to the Ivory Coast. I wondered if it was worth it, especially when a Black person calls you a "fucking African" and tells you to "go back to your jungle country". I was completely shocked by these types of comments coming from a Black person toward another Black person. If it was a White person, I would feel he had said it because he was racist, but this was a Black person calling me names when I was just doing my job. I just smiled and carried on with my work. Those ignorant people see Africa as a country not a continent. Please, God, forgive them; they do not know where they come from and what they are doing. I really do not understand why Black people hate others of their own race so much. We Blacks are the most oppressed in the world, we are supposed to unite and help each other. Instead we enjoy belittling each other. What a shame and an embarrassment.

The more I'm settling down slowly in my new country, the more I understand how the system works. What surprises me the most is the power of the media, especially the TV channels. These TV channels are so powerful they can influence bringing down any government in power. These TV channels have so much freedom, they can talk about anything within the law of the country (as long as it's not compromising the security of the country) compared to the channels in Africa who promote only the positive values of the current government. African channels cannot dare criticise the current government. Any African who wants to know how democracy is applied in politics needs to follow Western politics. The ruling party is constantly under pressure, constantly under criticism to improve the economy, the security and well-being of the population. The ruling party and opposition political party argues, challenging each other to do better if elected. European countries are constantly building, progressing, improving and maintaining what they have already done. Western politicians have their differences as anywhere in the world but during a period of crises like war, terrorist attacks, flooding or economy meltdown etc., all politicians put aside their differences and work together, put their forces together to defend, protect or save their country. That is what I called democracy. When the country is attacked by terrorists (rebels) no politicians will defend or justify what these terrorists have done. All political parties with one voice will condemn and will do whatever it takes to give all power to the ruling party to defend the country and severely punish terrorists.

The second surprise I noticed is the image of Africa these Western TV channels project on their screen. The images these Western channels show on their screens are always negative, ugly, very bad images about African countries. For these Western channels there are never good things about Africa always, always bad. Whatever it is – a documentary or news about Africa, they always show deaths of children in their thousands caused by malnutrition. You can see always war where Africans are killing each other day in and day out. They show the lack of basic elements for the population such as no electricity, no clean water, no roads, no decent housing. As an African I'm shocked, angry and confused because I know that not everywhere is like that in African countries – they are poor but it's not every part of each African country that lacks electricity and lacks decent housing. Western media plays a very good role in feeding the beliefs of racists.

As an African man in a foreign country, everything you see on the TV you constantly watch negative images of your continent and you are not happy. You constantly watch a young child covered in dust and walking miles and miles on a dusty road without shoes, collecting water, water shared by animals to take home to be used as drinking water. You constantly see news about Africa where people are dying in their thousands because their own government cannot feed them and relies on Western generosity for food.

England is the best country in Europe but black people are still victims of discrimination; racism is everywhere. When you are not in your own country you must accept everything that is thrown at you with pride, dignity, determination and keep yourself safe and have a life.

Africans are not all talented to be footballers and make massive amounts of money. Africans are not all talented to be athletes. Some, like me, wanted to use their intellect to make a living. Unfortunately, no matter how much experience you have, no matter your degree or how good your qualification is, you are not trusted enough to do intellectual work.

I travelled a lot in Europe and believe me or not, life in England for an African person is far, far better than any other European country. At least British people allow us to be educated and give us some jobs, even if it is not what you want but you have a job which can allow you to feed your family. You have to be grateful in life.

Why do black people, especially Africans, have to suffer in this world? What have Africans have done to people on this planet to be constantly humiliated and frustrated?

One day, I finished my job and was so tired I just wanted to go home. The nearest train station was seven minutes from the hospital where I worked. My train journey ended at Finsbury Park Station where I intended to get the 253 or 254 bus to go home. I was at the bus stop waiting for my bus when a white man came up to me and spat on my shoes. He turned and was about to leave when I grabbed him gently to get him to explain why he had done that. He just looked at me and said he hated Black people – he could not stand them. He also added that if he had the power, he would wipe out all Black people from this planet because, in his opinion, Blacks are useless, lazy parasites. Then from nowhere, he pushed me in the face. That is one thing I would never tolerate. We started fighting in front of a lot of people at the bus stop. Suddenly two of his friends got involved in the fight. Three men against one; I had no chance. I did not know whether to run for my life or stand up for myself and fight them all. What will happen will happen! I stood up to them but I was well beaten. I was lucky enough, and some people intervened to stop the one-way fight and another called the police. When they heard the police sirens approaching, the three White men ran away. I stood and waited for the police to see if they could catch the idiots that did this to me by checking all the surrounding surveillance cameras.

When the police arrived, they did not care about me, how I felt, if I needed an ambulance, or if I was okay. Their main concern was to find out whether I was an illegal immigrant, presumably so that I could be deported back to Africa. I was shocked that police officers in a developed country like the United Kingdom, who were supposed to serve and protect citizens, did not do their job – or maybe it was because I am Black and all Blacks are supposed to be illegal immigrants until proven otherwise. After checking my date of birth, my address, and where I worked, as they found nothing suspicious on me, as I had no criminal record and as I was working legally, they let me go, saying that they would send me the police report by post. Regarding the crime of which I was the victim, they told me that nothing could be done because there were no cameras in that zone. I had just been beaten for no reason and nobody would be charged with the crime.

No matter how badly I was treated by those English policeman I would never blame all English people. The English accept you in their country, they allow you to be educated and give you shelter, money to feed yourself and all the help needed to be to be integrated into their society. In fact, I'm grateful to the English people. There are always a small and ignorant minority who spoil the name and reputation of a great country like the United Kingdom. We Africans love the British for their fairness, their sense of justice and humanism. As a black person when I see the great jobs some black people are doing in England (judges, ministers, MPs, managers of great companies, GPs and consultants etc...) I'm always and will always thank God for letting me be in this great country.

What could I do as an African man in Europe? I just picked myself up, dusted myself off, collected the bag and keys I had dropped on the ground during the fight, took my bus, and went home. Though I had blood on my face and arm and felt in bad shape, at least I had survived. On my way home, a few ideas went through my mind. What if I had been an illegal immigrant who was beaten up, stabbed, or knocked down by a car and had broken bones? Would they have deported me after I had received treatment in a hospital? I will never know. What if I had been a female illegal immigrant who had been raped and tortured? Would they have deported me after finding out I did not have the right to stay in this country even though I had been the victim of a vicious crime? What if it were three Blacks who had beaten up one White man? Would the police have behaved in the same way, or would the whole area of Finsbury Park have been patrolled by the police in order to catch the offenders? I did not know. The next day I went to work as if nothing had happened. This is life in Europe.

I am just one of millions of Africans who felt compelled to leave their countries for a better life in Europe. My life is not that important, but if my children, my grandchildren, and my great-grandchildren are forced to leave their motherland in Africa to find a better life in Europe and they have to go through the same hell I'm going through, then forgive me, my Lord, I will say that I came into this world for no reason.

Africans are suffering because our so-called leaders do nothing to improve our lives; that's why many of us end up in Europe. We come to Europe because there are no jobs in Africa; the few jobs that are available are sold to those who can afford them. We have very little security or law and order in Africa. At least in Europe, an African can work and make a little money to take care of his or her family. In Europe you can go to school, college, or university to further your education. In Europe you have the ability to feed yourself and your family on a regular basis. We Africans are not in Europe because we want to be here, but because our leaders, by their ineptitude, cruelty and corruption, force us to leave our countries to find a better life elsewhere, and that is mainly in Europe.

During the period of slavery, Westerners would go to Africa to buy Africans to work in their plantations in Europe or America. Nowadays, in this twenty-first century, it is us Africans who are begging the West to let us into their countries to have jobs so that we can feed our families. What type of jobs are we doing, anyway? It's the same old jobs our great-grandparents were doing during the time of slavery. The only difference is that this time we use modern appliances. In fact, slavery has not really been abolished; it is just the way African people are now trafficked into Europe or America that has changed. What can an African do once he or she is in Europe after the sacrifices made by their parents to pay for their ticket? Some parents are prepared to borrow huge sums of money or sell their home, their livestock, their clothing, and all their valuables to pay for a ticket for their child so that he or she can have a good education in Europe. A good education means a good job. It is every parent's dream in Africa to have a child who is educated in Europe. Having a child in Europe brings an African family honour, respect, and envy in their community, especially when that child returns and buys them a decent house and things they could not have afforded if that child had stayed in Africa. Going back home uneducated or with no money would be a humiliation, an embarrassment, not just to yourself but also to your family. How will your parents pay back the money they borrowed or replace the goods they sold? How are you going to explain to them why you were deported? Europe is, for most Africans, a dream land. Once you are in Europe, you cannot just go back because you are not strong enough to take the racist comments, the humiliation, the bullying, and the harassment; you must swallow your pride and your dignity to reach your goal.

African parents, if you are mentally prepared for your daughters to be prostitutes, if you want your children to be cleaners, chambermaids, labourers in farms or factories, or kitchen porters, you can send them to Europe, unless you have enough money to take care of their studies, their rent, and everything they need to survive during their stay in Europe. How can you go to work with fear in your stomach because you do not have the right papers which would allow you to work legally? How can educated men or women, who have decent jobs in Africa leave their jobs, for cleaning or chambermaid jobs in Europe? So many African people are in prison because the desire to make big money quickly drives them to commit crimes. So many among them are killed, with no one knowing, no one caring. Very few Africans make it. Only those who have the right papers, can get a decent education, and manage to have decent jobs, but even they struggle to make a decent living because they have to take care of many family members back in Africa. If you want to bet your life on coming to Europe, it's your choice; at least you should know what awaits you.

We Africans are treated like slaves and always will be; when you take on one hand the quality of life in Western countries and on the other hand the quality of life in Africa, you can see there is no comparison. The quality of life in Western countries is far, far better than that in Africa. This is why racism will always exist.

Our great-grandparents were slaves, our parents were slaves, and we are slaves. There are two types of slavery: there is the physical slavery under which our great grandparents wasted their lives, and we as Black Africans in this twenty-first century are suffering of the second type, the most savage type of slavery, which is financial and moral slavery.

When I was growing up, I was told that the West is a dream land, a land of prosperity, peace, and opportunity. In Africa, to be considered as 'civilized' you must dress, eat, talk, and behave like a Westerner. Since I was a child, when I saw movies on television, I always saw white people with nice houses, eating nice meals, driving nice cars, and wearing nice clothes. I envied them and dreamt one day to be there in Europe to taste happiness, to live like them. I grew up with the idea that the White race was the race of God; it was a blessed race because God gave them everything they needed to make them happy. In contrast, I saw Africans as a race cursed by God with starvation, disease, warmongers, rapists, and killers of women and babies.

As I grew up, I went to school, then to college and finally to university. While I was going through my education, I realized the ideas I used to have about European countries and African countries were false. In fact, Western countries used to have leaders as bad as African leaders of today. They were corrupt, greedy, selfish and evil. The West used to have selfish leaders who spared little thought for the poor and weak. In the distant past, most European states were controlled by absolutist monarchies. The Western countries, for significant parts of their histories, were ravaged by war, starvation and diseases. The men, women, children and old people in the Western countries at that time were dying in their thousands every day from the poor living conditions – the same conditions that African people are living in at the moment. As time went by however, the people began to decide enough was enough. They decided they could not go on living like savages in their own countries, while a small minority were living like gods and goddesses. In some countries their population came together to demand better living conditions, justice for all, access to education, healthcare, decent housing for all no matter how poor or rich you were etc. The rich and the powerful refused, of course; they called in the security forces to oppress and intimidate. They bribed some, even killed those who dared challenge their authority. In some countries the poor refused to back down and were prepared to die if necessary. No matter how ruthless you are, you cannot kill or imprison every single human being in your country. The pace and process of change varied from country to country. Eventually they were rich and powerful statesmen who came to accept the need for reform. Despite all the conflict, the rich, the powerful and the poor began to put aside their differences. Over time, there was some redistribution of wealth and legal reforms to improve the living conditions for the population, and to enhance equality of opportunity. Lessons were learned so that past mistakes would not be repeated. Improved living conditions for the general population enhances the stability, peace and progress of the motherland. Nobody wants to die but to avoid having to live in unacceptably poor conditions, I would rather die fighting for better conditions for myself, my children and my grandchildren than do nothing and just hope for the best. Expecting that, through prayers one day everything will be OK with God's help. God gave us all everything we need to be successful, prosperous and happy. God gave us good health, the desire to know, to learn, to understand, to investigate, to create and to enjoy. God gave us knowledge and an abundance of natural resources to survive. Do not expect God to put food on your table when you are too lazy to move your ass to find a job when jobs are available. Prayers only will not bring stability, progress, peace, better living conditions and equal opportunity. You can pray as much as you want and as long as you want, but without teachers, builders and farmers respectively your children will not be taught and educated, your building will not be built and you will not have food at your market.

Westerners have what they have (stability, progress, better living conditions etc…). Things we Africans want because they worked hard to obtain it. God has nothing to do with it. Their great-grandparents sacrificed their lives to make sure their great-grandchildren would live in peace, prosperity, and stability. They designed systems in which, as far as possible, it is ensured their leaders work for the people, and not just for themselves or for their families or friends. The Western leaders designed a system in which each citizen has the opportunity to obtain decent housing, a decent education, a decent job, justice, and freedom for all, regardless of ethnic, religious, or economic background.

What is happening in Africa: war (Muslims against Christians, Christians against Muslims or different ethnic groups killing each other), coups d'état will not be tolerated in Europe because European countries build structure for peace and stability. The citizens of Western countries have learnt to respect their laws and constitution blindly. No one will take power by force and no one backed by any foreign power will be allowed to become president or prime minister.

Any worker, no matter how much you earn, will pay taxes and these taxes will be used to build roads, hospitals, colleges or universities. If you are not in a job your government will look after you by giving you some financial help (money for food, free medication when sick) until you find a job.

We Africans can live like they do in the West; we need to believe in ourselves and learn to love ourselves and each other. To achieve the same quality of life as that which exists in the West, we must get rid of all corrupt leaders and their associates peacefully or by force. We must work as hard as the West and prove to the rest of the world that Africans are not the inferior race that people such as the American scientists think. We Africans have the ability and the intelligence to participate in the development of this planet. We cannot live like parasites that always depend on the West hand out. We have what we need to be as powerful as the West. It is true that many African countries were colonized by the West, but that is not an excuse for the inability of our current leaders to provide a better life for their people. In fact, the crimes committed by the West during the colonization period are nothing, I repeat, nothing, compared to the crimes committed by Blacks on other Blacks in this day and age. I do not need to provide any proof; it is plain to see from what is going on in Africa between Africans and in the rest of the world between Blacks. We Blacks, no matter where we are on this planet, love to hate each other.

Why are we Africans content to blame the West for the wars in Africa? The West is not totally responsible for our miserable lives. The West is not entirely responsible for the way our leaders govern our people. We Africans are responsible, no one else. When war breaks out in a particular country in Africa, who is seen with guns? Who is seen killing? Who is seen stealing? Who is seen raping women, no matter how old they are? It's us Africans. It's true that the weapons used are provided by the West. We Africans are so divided it makes it so easy for the West to control us, control our leaders and our natural resources.

We Africans are not animals. When somebody asks you to go and kill your own people, you have the right to say no, no matter what the West promises you. So why do we blame other people for what we do to ourselves? Maybe we are not as intelligent as we think we are. Maybe we love being called savages tamed by the West who, because they do not want our countries to be militarily, financially, and politically strong like their countries, recruit mercenaries, most of them African, give them the best weapons, the best military training guided by the best instructors money can buy and send them into their chosen countries in Africa (countries with an abundance of natural resources) to destroy us. I grew up believing that God gave all human beings the ability to do whatever they want as long as they put their minds to it. Honestly speaking, I think we Africans have a problem. I went to university, I read a lot of books, and nowhere have I ever read of an African country, no matter how rich, that has recruited mercenaries to bring about a coup d'état in a European country. It is always African countries that are the victims of coup d'états initiated by the West. How can we expect the rest of the world to respect our people if our leaders cannot provide the basic conditions of existence? How do we expect the rest of the world to see us as equals if our countries cannot compete with the West in terms of quality of living, technology, and science? How do we expect racism to be abolished when we Blacks are proving to the rest of the world that we cannot stop killing each other like savages? At this rate, if we do not stop killing each other, in five hundred years there will be no Black people left on this planet.

A family of lions in the bush is always led by a dominant male. That dominant male will do whatever it takes to keep his title. If there are any challengers, the dominant male will fight to the death; he will either win and force the challenger into exile or die and lose his title. Either way, there are no rules of succession. If you are a leader, you will remain a leader until you encounter someone stronger who kicks you out (a coup), or you will die a leader and a battle will begin among the pretenders to your crown (a civil war). This example explains exactly how democracy works in Africa. Sometimes when a leader starts feeling his age, he gives the power to his son or corrupts the army into backing his son.

So when he dies, the son becomes the next commander-in-chief. No one will try to kill him or snatch back from his family the wealth he has stolen from his poor people.

Please, God, tell me what is wrong with us Africans. From generation to generation, our lives have not improved. We live like mad people in Africa, where the most powerful rule the land. Africans should not be regarded as less intelligent than others just because they have dictators as leaders. We Africans have what the West wants (immense natural resources), and the West has what we want (technology and science); why not sit down and trade? We cannot eternally be beggars who cannot live without the help of the West. The West has its own problems. Western leaders cannot ignore the needs of their people in order to please us Africans, that idea is unthinkable. Western leaders will always put the needs of their own people first, even if they must let all Africans die. Who can blame them? We Africans blame the West for killing us, but at the same time, we need them, to live. We Africans are begging Western countries to open their borders so that we can come in to better our lives. What a contrast! Our medicine is provided by the West. Our technology (cars, telephones, televisions, computers, etc.) comes from Western countries. Please wake up, Africa; make your children proud, and make us proud! The whole world is laughing at us!

African leaders, what do you want? Do you want to live and let your people die, or die and let your people live? African countries are not kingdoms where a king hands over his power to his favourite son. African countries are not cooperatives or companies in which the owner's eldest son takes over after the death of his father. Tell me, proud African people: How many people do you need to unseat a head of state who is incapable of protecting you against the atrocities of civil war; who is incapable of providing work, security, and healthcare for you; who believes that if he tries to bring stability, prosperity, education, and jobs, the West will want to kill him by creating a rebellion against his government? How many people do you need to depose a president who changes the constitution of the country to remain president for the rest of his life? These idiot presidents of African countries use colonisation to justify their incapacity to bring peace and development to their countries. Tell me, proud African people: How many people do you need to overthrow the head of the army who, instead of protecting the country, uses all the resources at his disposal to protect a useless government and keep a useless president in power? How many people do you need to remove from power a leader of a political party who does not work for the welfare of the country but uses his political party to divide the country and bring civil war (religious, ethnic, or tribal/caste)? How many people do you need to unseat these useless ministers who, instead of working for you proud Africans, to make your lives easier and better, use all the resources available to them to 'feed' their bank accounts in Europe so that their children and their descendants will have a better future while you proud Africans cannot afford a meal a day? How many people do you need to punish army officers who betrayed or gave up on their country during war?

These presidents, ministers, MPs, and mayors were elected to serve and protect the people. We did not elect them to make our lives miserable. We did not elect them to steal from us. We did not elect them to leave us in the mud, in rubbish, giving us scraps of food while their families and themselves enjoy good lives. We did not elect them to engage our countries in wars that never end. Any minister, mayor, or MP who is not fit to do the job for which they were elected must be forced out and replaced by a person of greater ability.

We Africans cannot talk about independence because we are not independent. How can we talk about independence when our leaders cannot provide for the basic needs of the people? How can you talk about being independent when African countries cannot 'breathe' without a handout of the West? We Africans will be independent when our leaders are able to provide shelter for everyone. We will be independent when law and order are enforced, irrespective of religion, ethnicity, tribe, or caste. We will be independent the day poor and rich Africans are judged under the same law without partiality; the day all Africans are able to provide for and regularly feed themselves and their families; the day poor and rich children have the same opportunity for jobs; the day African people are able to freely choose their own leaders without the interference of any foreign power. The day we are able to choose our religion without fear of persecution. The day we are able to protect and defend our country without the interference of the West, we Africans can say we are independent.

Life is too priceless to sacrifice it for a president or a political party leader who thinks only of his own gain. When a president is able to provide everything cited above, then we Africans will be happy to sacrifice our lives for him or her. Why should we fear death? Look at the West: Do you know how many people died during the First and Second World Wars protecting and defending their countries? Do you know how many people are still dying to make a better life for the next generation? No human being is immortal. Whether we want to or not, one day we will die. If you have to die to protect someone who is working for the country rather than his ethnic group, tribe, caste, or friends, so be it!

In the name of democracy, stability, progress, freedom of speech and religion, African terrorists backed by Western countries and renamed as rebels, brutally attacked their country with the best weapons money can buy, weapons the army of their own country cannot afford to buy, because Western countries do not want the current president. The current president who refuses to obey to the dicta of Western countries. A leader who put the need of his/her country first and refused to sacrifice the life of his/her people to satisfy the greed of Western companies.

War is a very expensive and messy business. These rebels backed by their Western allies are more powerful politically, have more money therefore can recruit more mercenaries, more warmongers in their ranks and are well-organised.

These Africans rebels (most of the time these are the most ignorant people who come from the poorest families with no education) who for one reason or another recruit mercenaries. This is usually done with the help of foreign powers, starting a war in their own country, killing as many as possible, raping, stealing what they can, and burning the few buildings we have. Suddenly, these idiots become ministers or prime ministers, and sometimes when they kill more people, they become the head of state. What message is that giving to young children? The message that comes across is: You do not need to go to school, you do not need to go to university, you do not need to be the best student in your classroom, and you do not need to demonstrate to your people that you are capable of holding a ministerial post or leading a political party. What you need to do is be a rebel, recruit the best mercenaries with the help of European countries and start the destruction of your own country because you are not happy with the current government. Finally, if you kill many of your people, you can be a minister, a prime minister, or even a president of the republic. The reward is too great to ignore. That is why our Africa will always 'bleed': because there is no law and order. Anyone can be the head of state, no matter their background; a killer, a rapist, a thief can be president.

How can you forgive, collaborate with, or even ask for financial help from a rebel, leader or not, who during the war burned your people alive, made people eat the flesh of their murdered relatives. Forced you to watch your daughter, mothers, sisters, nieces being gang-raped. Forced boys to rape their own mothers, forced fathers to rape their own daughters, forced grandchildren to rape their own grandmothers, placed bets on the sex of a foetus and then disembowelled pregnant women to find out who had won? Your babies are being raped; people are sick. Boys and girls lived through the war and were neglected by their parents because they were just trying to survive. How can you live with yourself when the person who did that to you has become your minister, prime minister, or president? Do you have any dignity left? Do you have any honour left inside your soul? A curse on those who have any link with these savages; a curse on those who will eat at the same table with them; a curse on those women who will share their bed with them; a curse on those who will be united with them through marriage; a curse on those who will work for them; a curse on those who will take orders from them and obey them. Punishing these savages will be as legitimate as paying your taxes. These idiots think they are the only people who know how to love and protect their own siblings. But they do so while they are hurting others. How do you expect your child to look you in the eyes and call you father, mother or granny after what these poor innocent children were forced to endure?

Most of these idiot rebels come from deprived areas, but once they are in power, they do not care about the deprivation of their people and think they can do as they please. Who can blame them? That is why war must be avoided at all costs. If political leaders do not understand that sentiment, it means they are not fit to lead the country. Before you go to war, make sure you know how much you are willing to lose. You do not go to war because someone hurts the feelings of the president or a political leader; you do not go to war because you want to prove to the world you are the strongest. You do not go to war against your own country because it is the only way for you to become a minister, prime minister, or president. You go to war to fight and protect your motherland. You go to war for your rights, your freedom. You go to war when your women, parents, and children are treated like livestock anyone can buy and sell. You go to war because you want freedom, equality, justice for all and decent living conditions for yourself and your family.

African countries are not the only countries that were victims of the atrocities of colonisation. Consider Malaysia, India, and China. Malaysia and India got their independence from the British, but China fought a bloody war to get their freedom from Japan. After becoming free, they picked themselves up and reorganised themselves, and today their people are enjoying the benefits of the hard work of their grandparents. Even if these countries do not have the same high standard of living as Western countries, progress has been made, and they are still progressing. No foreign army can go into these countries to organise a coup. No foreign government can go into these countries and tell them which leader they need as their president. The leaders of these countries design a system to care for their people; these leaders want progress and stability, for the well-being of their people. None of the African countries can compete with these countries in terms of technology, stability, and progress made so far. We Africans need stability and peace, and to have that, we need a very good structure based on our tradition and culture, a very strong leadership and above all unity.

Bangne Plan:

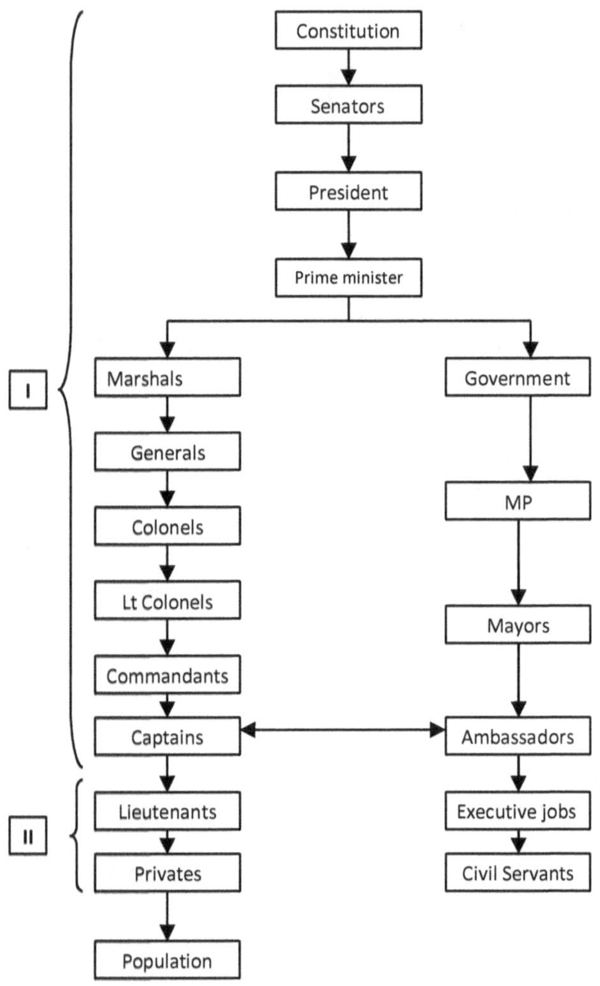

I.   Occupants of these jobs must fulfil one of these conditions:

. Hard core nationalist.

. If married to a member of the same ethnic, religious, tribe or caste group; both must be a descendant of families that have had the same nationality for four generations.

. If married to a member of a different ethnic, religious, tribe or caste group; both must be a descendant of families that have had the same nationality for two generations.

II.   Occupants of these jobs must fulfil one of these conditions:

. Married to a member of the same ethnic, religious, tribe or caste group; both must be a descendent of families that have had the same nationality for two generations.

. Married to a member of a different ethnic, religious, tribe or caste group; both must be a descendant of families that have had the same nationality for one generation.

If you are from an ethnic, tribe group A, your partner must be from an ethnic, tribe group A otherwise your family will do whatever it takes to break up your relationship (intimidations, lies, warning, ultimatum etc…). The same goes for religious, tribe or caste groups. Many families have been broken or forced to go their separate ways because a person's partner is not from their ethnic, religious, tribal, or caste group. Many people fall in love with someone and think they have found their dream partner for life, but they cannot get together because they are from different ethnic, religious, tribal or caste groups. There are some parts of Africa where people are born with the title of high ethnic, religious, tribal, or caste group, and some with a lower ethnic, religious, tribal, or caste group. If you are not lucky enough to be born into a higher ethnic, tribal or caste group, there are some posts you will not be allowed to hold, no matter how intelligent you are. People suffer discrimination because of their ethnic, religious, tribal, or caste group, and that discrimination increases tension between different groups. When the opportunity arises for the victims of discrimination to get their revenge against the group that is responsible for all their humiliation and discrimination, the killing starts, especially during and after an election. We must avoid that by breaking these prejudices. The only way to break these prejudices is to allow relationships or marriages between different groups to blossom without the interference of any family members. This will help people come to accept others' ethnicities, religions, tribes, or castes as part of their cultural values.

How to choose senators

Each country in Africa is made up of different towns; around each town, we have villages. Each village is composed of different areas; each area is made up of different families and each family is led by the head of the family. To be head of a family, you must be married. The heads of each family must gather to choose their leaders.

The leader of each family must fulfil these conditions:

Have the most wisdom, be the most respected, be the one to whom the people listen, and be the most trusted.

Be able to write, read, and fluently speak the national language and know the culture and tradition inside out.

Be able to convince his people to put the interests of the country before their own privileges and desires (these could be ethnic, religious, tribal, caste group or individual family interests).

The leaders of each family must gather to choose the head of the village.

The head of the village must:

Unite the village. In case of any rancour between families, any division, any misunderstanding, he should be able to judge without partiality. He must be fair and honest.

Promote democracy. He must not force his people to vote for a political party based on religion, ethnicity, tribe, caste, or family relation. People must be free to choose or vote for any political party of their choice without the interference of anyone (family members, friends, etc).

The heads of each village in each town must gather to elect a senator. The senator must be chosen according to the laws of democracy.

The Role of the Senators

Each senator must be able to unite all the villages of his town.

The senators must have the power to make sure witchcraft is used only for the defence of the villages, the towns, and the country in case of war. Witchcraft may also be used for scientific, medical, and technological research. The senators must design a system to judge witchcraft. Anyone who is found guilty of using witchcraft for a harmful purpose, such as putting a curse on someone, killing or injuring someone, must be severely punished. The punishment of the first person caught must be used as a warning to those who might be tempted to use their power to hurt people.

The senators must be able to unite all the ethnicities, tribes, or caste groups of the country as one. They must have all the power they need to maintain peace, stability, harmony, and mutual respect among all the ethnicities, tribes, or caste groups for the well-being of their citizens.

The power of the senators must be based on the constitution of the country. The constitution of each country must be based on its tradition, culture, and history. We can also use suitable constitutions from various democratic countries such as America and Canada or Germany. We may select laws that can fit into our traditions and culture, but any law that is contradictory to our culture, traditions and way of life must be rejected.

The senators must have sufficient powers to control the government and to ensure the constitution is followed. They (the senators, the government and all the opposition parties) must work together not to allow a foreign army to land in their country. They (senators, government and all the opposition parties) must work together to stop or give any excuses to a foreign power to use a political party as a cover to organize a coup. This is to prevent any foreign power from trying to force their president, who is working hard to bring stability, encourage progress, create jobs, and unite the country, to go into exile because he is putting the needs of his people first. They cannot allow a foreign power to tell them which president is good for them and which is not. Senators must not give a foreign power, such as a Western nation, any excuse to land by force in their country to stage a coup, because Western countries have an abundance of power (political, economical and military).

The Armed and police Forces: The formation of an army and police officers is not just a matter of selecting the strongest men and women, putting Kalashnikovs into their hands and sending them out on to the battlefield. In this twenty-first century, the power of an army is not based only on the physical strength of the soldiers but also on their attitude and conduct (we do not need soldiers who can be bought to betray their own country), their courage, their love of their country, and above all on the technology available to them. None of the African countries have the military technology to effectively resist the armed forces of Western countries.

Finance: Western countries have the strongest economies. This is the reason why so many Africans are prepared to die to live in Europe.

Politics: The United Nations backs and will always back Western countries attempting to force (using civil or military measures) any African country to obey their demands. Given the opportunity, Western countries will do whatever they wish to any African country. The only way to avoid a foreign army landing by force in one's own African country is to ensure the Government observes the provisions of the country's constitution, the rules of democracy. These provisions should empower senators to prevent a president from changing the constitution so that he or she can remain in power for life. They must put the needs of their people first. The power must be in the hands of their people. It is only the people who will decide who must lead them, nobody else. The will of the people must be respected at all costs. Anyone working to destroy democracy must be dealt with severely, regardless of who they are, their job title, or whether they have the support of the West or not.

How to Choose Political Leaders:

In African countries, having both sizeable Christian and Muslim populations, the president of the republic must have two main advisers: One must be the national leader of the Muslim community, and the other must be the national leader of the Christian community. The leaders of these two communities must have all the powers they need to maintain peace, stability, harmony, and mutual respect between Muslims and Christians for the well-being of the country and its citizens. These two leaders must collaborate with the senators to create a committee that has the power to make sure the president and his ministers do not abuse the constitution and work for the well-being of the nation. They must have the power to impeach the ministers or the president if they are not respecting the constitution or are not working to bring progress, stability, and peace. We Africans do not want any religious wars. In the case of any wrongdoing (corruption, abuse of power, taking or giving bribes, or any breach of the constitution) from either the Muslim leader or the Christian leader, it will be only the Muslim or Christian community that has the power to remove their representative according to the law of democracy. The president, the government, and the army must not have the power to remove either of them.

How to choose the national leaders of Muslims and Christians:

Each town has both a mosque and a church. Each mosque is led by an imam and each church is led by a pastor or priest.

To be an imam or priest/pastor, you must fulfil these conditions:

. Must be wise and pious and fear God
. Must be a model to follow

. Must avoid involvement in any political activity inside or outside the mosque or church. These places are holy sites for the worship of God only, not for engaging in politics or for encouraging one person to attack another because of their ethnicity, tribe, caste, religion, or alliance with an opposing political party of the majority in that church or mosque.

The representatives of each mosque and church must gather to choose their respective leaders of the town. The Muslim leader and Christian leader of each town in the country must gather to choose their respective national leader who will be the advisor of the president. The leaders of the mosques and churches of each town, each village and each province must gather to design a system that will make it difficult to have a religious war. In these churches and mosques, the leaders have the duty and responsibility to make sure Muslim and Christians can live together in peace and harmony as one community, no matter where they are in the country.

Each town must be governed and represented by two people: a mayor and a Member of Parliament (MP). Both must be from the same political party. The MP's job is to ensure the constitution is fully respected. The mayor's first job is to ensure the town is clean: no dead bodies in the street, refuse collected regularly, no people with mental disabilities walking naked in the street, etc. Secondly, the mayor must be responsible for all matters related to the town's finances, including who pays their taxes and who does not, how many people are unemployed, how much money in taxes his town generates, etc. We need to copy the example of the West (America, Canada, and England) of how their towns are governed and organised. The roles being performed by the mayors and the MPs of each town must be supervised by the respective senators of each town.

Each year, each town performances must be published. The performance must be based on the quality of life (crime and cleanliness), the timekeeping, the professionalism of all employees and employers. The population of each town needs to know how the authorities work to reduce the numbers of complaints made by the members of public. The people need to know which town of the country enforced the country constitution very well. Each town must fight very hard to have zero tolerance against corruption, xenophobia, racism, favouritism and religious extremism.

For democracy to work efficiently, we need a small and fixed political party system. A person cannot be in a political party at the beginning and then, because he is not happy with his leader at the time, leave his first party and create another party. Political parties in Africa tend to be created like small companies are created in Europe. It can almost seem like there are more political parties in one town than people who live there. That is a joke. All too often, people create political parties, not to represent and defend the weak and poor, but to negotiate with the ruling party for some administrative posts for themselves, their family and their followers. We need five to eight political parties in each country, no more.

During a presidential election, each party must provide five candidates: one from the north of the country, one from the south, one from the east, one from the west, and one from the centre. None of the candidates must come from the same ethnic, tribal, or caste group as the last president.

We need a system that is fair and just for anyone who is fit to lead the country. The last thing we need is for a leader of a political party to accuse the system of being xenophobic. We do not want it said for example that "They do not want me to be president because I'm Christian, Muslim, from the

West, etc." The consequences of such accusations can be fatal and can cause a needless religious or ethnic war. We Africans cannot afford any more war.

Once each political party has chosen its five candidates, the senators will then take the candidates' names from each party to every village and town of their province. Each village or province will choose one candidate from each party. The chosen candidate will then represent his party in the next presidential election. Those who believe in God must pray that God will guide them to make the best choice. For those who think they can use their mystic powers, so be it, as long as the best candidate is chosen. The best candidate is not necessarily someone who is related to you or someone from your ethnic, religious, tribe or caste group but someone who, once in power, will bring prosperity, happiness, joy, and unity to the country; someone who will bring peace, progress, democracy, and stability; someone who will respect the constitution and make sure the constitution is respected; someone who will enforce law and order. African countries need someone who is prepared to feed his people first and be ready to die if necessary, to protect the interests and the natural resources of his country. We Africans do not want a cursed individual who, once in power, will bring division and increase the misery of the people. We Africans do not want someone who, once in power, will bring war with all the atrocities that follow. African people do not want someone who will use religious, ethnic and tribal differences as a weapon to stay in power forever. The development of Africa is in our hands. No one else will die for our freedom. No one will come and make our lives better. We cannot keep blaming the West for helping us kill our people.

Before the committee starts counting the votes, each representative of each political party must sign an agreement to show that they are satisfied with the way the election was organized. This agreement must be supervised by all the senators of the country. If there are any disagreements and the complainant can prove or justify why he or she is not happy, the election must be reorganized by taking into account the comments of the others; everybody must be satisfied before the election organizers can start counting the votes. Before the results are published, an agreement must also be signed stating that everyone will accept the results, even if they lose, so that accusations of cheating are not made. The senators must prevent anyone from proclaiming victory before they start counting the votes or before they have the results of the election. If a candidate signs the agreement stating that they are happy with the way the election took place, but then want to bring catastrophe to the country because they lost, the senators must have enough power to deal with them. Even the death sentence would be appropriate, for these leaders who do not care about the people but themselves. Killing a few idiots to save millions of people in the country may be a necessary evil.

The senators must have enough power to unite all the ethnic, tribal, or caste groups of the country. The senators must have the duty and responsibility of enforcing law and order and making sure each person can marry someone outside their ethnic, tribal, or caste group in peace and harmony without the interference of any family members. They must have the power to create a system in which it will be difficult or impossible to have any ethnic, tribal, or caste war in the country. In the case of any chaotic trouble between any groups, the senators, the president, the army, and the government of the country must deal with it together as soon as possible before more lives are lost. They must find out who is responsible and punish them severely, no matter who they are or what post they occupy, according to the laws of democracy and make sure no more of these troubles will occur in the future for the sake and stability of the country. The West cannot invest in a country that is not stable. No stability, no development.

When we talk about development, we are talking about economic, social, political, and military development.

Before any election (presidential, mayoral, or MP), each candidate of each political party must provide their manifesto (a description of what they will do for the country and for the people if they win the election). Once in power, these promises must be fully carried out. Anyone who fails to fulfil their promises to the people must not be allowed to participate in the next election; no excuses or blame games for losers or liars. Any political opposition that tries to use illegality or ferment violence to disrupt the work of the ruling party, no matter the reason, must be banished for many years. Any ruling party which creates their own problems and tries to blame others must be ejected from power. Any punishment must be carried out in public, according to the law of democracy, by the senators only. We Africans are already behind the wagon of progress. We do not need politicians who are only good speakers or conjurers.

To be president you must:

When your party wins the election , you become president of the republic.
As president, you need maximum of two terms, no more.

Belong to a
Political party
(Member or head)

When your party win you become president.
Maximum two term no more.

When your party loose the election, You can represent your Party for the next election with the blessing of the Members.

When your party loose the election you must be replaced by someone else, no matter how rich or good you are. Did not belong to someone For Life.

How to Choose Ministers

Each political party must have its government ready.

Each political party (opposition or ruling party) must have the same number of ministers.

Each ethnicity, tribe, or caste must be represented in each ministerial post of each political party.

It's forbidden to give a ministerial post to more than one person of the same ethnic, tribal, or caste group. We must avoid any favour toward or discrimination against any ethnic, tribal, or caste group. We cannot have a situation in which, because the president or the minister is from ethnicity, tribe, or caste A, most of the ministers or the employees also come from ethnicity, tribe, or caste A, while the members of ethnicity, tribe, or caste B do not have any representatives in the government, even if they are the minority. We call that discrimination and xenophobic behaviour.

It's forbidden for any minister to give a job to someone who is related to him or his partner or someone from his ethnicity, tribe, or caste group. Any job, especially any ministerial job, must be given to the right person with the best knowledge.

It's forbidden for any minister to give a job to a relative or friend of another minister.

It's forbidden for two political parties to combine force against a ruling political party. Democracy in an Africa coalition cannot work. Each political party must fight to have the love, the trust and the vote of the population.

In case of any fraud or misbehaviour committed by a minister or civil servant, the police must investigate thoroughly in order to find out who is responsible and take the appropriate action according to the law, ensuring lessons are learned for the future so the mistakes will not be repeated.

Appointment to ministerial posts must be based on merit, and therefore these key posts should go to men and women who are well equipped intellectually, to do the best possible job.

There should be a fixed number (i.e. a quota) of women as ministers in each political party in the country. Women are certainly intellectually equipped to perform in political posts just as well as men. There is a tendency in Africa to regard women as being in this world just to make babies, cook the meals, and take care of the house. Part of the reason we Africans are in such a mess is because far fewer women are involved in politics than men.

The ambassadors that represent the African countries abroad must come from each ethnicity, tribe, or caste.

All the ministries of government (like Defence, Economy, Transport, Immigration, Health, Environment, Social Services, Education, Communication, Employment, Justice, etc.) must have the same structure as those of Western governments. We need to copy the best parts of the West's culture and combine them with our own traditions to make a better life for our people. We should not copy blindly what the West does, especially if some of their laws cannot fit into our system. We Africans have our own cultures and traditions, and we must not lose our identity.

United we can rebuild our planet Earth; divided we are all dead.

Some Africans have a dream: a dream to one day become an MP, a mayor, a minister, a prime minister, or even president. In Africa, the possession of power has had a corrupting influence on those who have achieved positions of power. Once these posts are occupied, it is as if the post holder becomes a god. They and their associates are untouchable. No law in the land can stop them from doing whatever they want to do. They and their associates can embezzle as much as they want so that they, their associates, and their families will never worry about money for the rest of their lives. They call themselves the representatives, the voice of the people. They send their idiot children to study in the best universities in Europe. Their children do not have to work and go through the hell that ordinary Africans in Europe have to go through because their parents have already paid for everything (university fees, rent, and healthcare insurance) plus a fat monthly cheque for pocket money. Meanwhile students from poor families in Africa cannot afford a pencil to do their homework. These people (presidents, prime ministers, ministers, MPs, mayors) do little or nothing to make life easier for the population they are supposed to be helping. When the money runs out in the country and they do not know how to pay the employees, these same people will then accuse the West of trying to suffocate the country's finances in order to provoke a rebellion against them.

After many years living in Europe, if you are lucky enough to have the opportunity, you may decide to go back home to Africa to create a small company. You may have to use most of your savings to hire one or two people, which would be a way for you to reduce unemployment and help reduce the misery of your people. Your good intentions are however, likely to turn into a nightmare because the relevant ministers will make your life so miserable you will change your mind and abandon the idea to create a company. From top to bottom, the staff of the administration will force you to pay them bribes before they can deliver the licence you require to start your business. Once you obtain your licence, you will have little or no money left to start your business. These Ministers are in effect saying to you, "These Africans do not need a job. Let them suffer; let them starve to death. We do not care about them; let them be unemployed so that we can use them when needed. Let them grow old without any skills as long as we ministers have enough money to take care of our families and send our children to Europe to continue their studies."

African countries are poor, and we need private companies, both large and small, to propel the economy forward. A government cannot create all the jobs needed for the population. To reduce unemployment, each government should help, facilitate, and encourage people who are willing to risk their savings to create small companies.

When God watches, he can only have pity for the way African people live and are treated by each other. Being forced to drink filthy water. Having to walk without shoes through the desert, bush, or forest during dry or wet seasons over long distances because they cannot afford the transport. Having to wear clothes pulled to pieces because they cannot afford new ones. Being obliged to live in a shanty-town without electricity or running water. When they get lucky, they can eat a handful of food a day; most of the time, they go to bed with empty stomachs. Parents were powerless to stop their children being violated. Families watched their relatives been burned alive. People were slaughtered like cattle for being Muslims, Christians or belonging to an ethnic group A or B. Poor and weak people were ignored and humiliated with no right in their own countries. Watch your people being consumed by diseases because they cannot afford hospital bills, etc.

God decides to send us, African people, a truly inspirational African leader. Someone who could pull our people from this misery, someone who wanted to restore democracy and transparency for the well-being of his people; someone who wanted to create jobs for everyone; someone who wanted everyone to have an education, decent housing, decent healthcare, freedom of speech, and freedom of religion; someone who could makes us feel human, someone who made us feel as if we could fulfil our dreams. Unfortunately some political leaders with the blessing and help of Western leaders would label him as a danger that must be stopped at any cost because he would want to force them to steal less. One morning you would learn that the new inspirational leader was either killed in a car or plane crash or was forced out by a military coup and replaced by the most corrupt among the corrupt. Instead of protecting our best men and women, instead of protecting those who are coming up with the best ideas to bring stability, democracy, and progress to our motherland, our so-called politicians see them as a danger and use all the means at their disposal to have them killed.

The difference between Africans and Europeans is that Europeans look after their intellectuals, their educated classes. These are people who are coming up with ideas that can propel their countries forward. It is like a few strong trees in the forest: the strength and the survival of the forest depends on these trees; therefore, if the forest is to prosper and grow from strength to strength, these trees must survive as long as possible until they are replaced. We all know we won't live forever, but you can live longer if you look after yourself. In these conditions, the West is prepared to tend the best trees and ensure they have enough nutrients to grow stronger. In Africa, our politicians cut down the stronger trees and we are left with the weak ones, and slowly but surely, the beautiful forest is disappearing.

What would you expect if you were to give your car keys to a blind person to drive you and your family through busy traffic? You would expect a crash, and when that crash happens, it would be no one's fault but your own. We Africans are in this whole mess because our leaders think the only way to acquire wealth and power is to please and have the blessing of Western governments. But Western governments do not care about freedom of speech, democracy, human rights or peace in Africa. Western governments do not care about how African countries are governed. What Western governments care about is to have a very good servant who will be prepared to 'starve' his/her people to 'feed' Western companies. We are being called savages because of these hypocrites; selfish and evil African leaders who relied on the military might of the West to stay in power indefinitely. One day a new and better servant will be selected by the West. Then the old servants will be replaced peacefully using a fake presidential election. A presidential election which the Western government already knows the winner. Or by force, either by a coup or rebellion created by the West.

If the West cares so much about democracy, peace, human rights and stability in Africa why is it, while Western governments crashed their terrorists all over the world, in Africa our terrorists labelled rebels are looked after, cared for, protected and help financially and military by Western government?

We are in a competitive world where each country wants to have the strongest economy, and the highest standard of living for their population. Each country wants to have the most powerful armed forces, the most effective political system, and the most advanced technology. For a nation to achieve these attributes, it needs to nurture, encourage and reward its best men and women. These men and women will be the innovators in society and will be the source of the best ideas for stability, enforcement of law and order, democracy, improvements in technology and science, etc. Such people can help a country to achieve excellence.

If our African politicians want their people to be at the bottom of the class, and their countries to be at the bottom of the league, they are going the right way about it.

If you want to, you can do it; if you do not want to, you will not do it. You must have the will and the desire to succeed, in order to achieve your goal.

Social Affairs

The social structure of many African societies is at the heart of all our pain. We Africans make babies, a lot of whom we cannot financially support. One cannot prevent a human being from having sex, but they need to know and understand that when they are not financially, emotionally, and physically ready, they should not have babies. Having a baby and then only being able to put food on the table is not enough – and anyway, many Africans cannot even manage that.

Consider a young girl growing up in a family where it's difficult for the family to feed her regularly because her father does not have regular employment. She may consider herself lucky if she can have one meal a day. Even if her father has a regular job, the poor man has so many people in his house to take care of that he would still be unable to provide optimal living conditions for his children. The poor girl wonders why she is on this planet and what to do to escape from her situation. At thirteen or fourteen, she notices some changes in her body and starts showing the signs of becoming an adult woman. She has bigger breasts than before, and her curves are now being noticed by men, who start staring at her with lust and desire. These men, including men the same age as her father or even older, may start giving her gifts and more money than she has ever had before. Suddenly she discovers that she can get whatever she wants from these men by giving them what they want – sex. Then she realizes she can make her dreams come true. She can buy any clothes, shoes, or make-up she wants to slap on and any food she wants to eat at any time she wants. The poor girl gets herself drawn into prostitution and she cannot see a way out without falling back into poverty. Involvement in prostitution brings its own problems such as unwanted pregnancies, sexually transmitted diseases, etc. So many talented girls in Africa destroy their futures at very young ages in this way because of their poverty. Boys can also have their prospects spoiled by poverty. Some turn to crime; for example, becoming drug dealers or master thieves. They may not be too fussy where they steal from (their own homes, neighbours' homes, friends' homes, farms, shops, etc.). They will steal anything they can sell, just to make a living.

A baby needs a loving and warm home with two devoted parents who are willing to make sacrifices for him or her. Shame on those children who cannot do better than their parents; shame on those parents who do not do everything in their power to make sure their children can have a better life than they. You cannot force a man and a woman to be together if they do not love each other as before, but they must put their differences aside for the children's sake even if they are separated.

An African family with five children is considered small. Many Africans regard having five children as the minimum. The story in so many African families is the same, no matter how rich or poor it is and no matter its location in Africa. Some couples have so many children, they cannot afford to take care of them, and therefore they leave them with the nearest member of their family in employment. Taking care of children means being able to feed them and take care of their school bills, health, transportation, and clothing. When you start a new job in Africa, you may end up with five to ten people in your house, even if you live in a one-bedroom flat with your partner. If you are an African living outside Africa (mainly Europe) you will be expected to send money home on a regular basis. These people are your relatives. When you live in Europe, your family left back home thinks of you as automatically being loaded with money. To them, someone who lives in Europe is better paid than most employees in Africa; therefore, you will be expected to send money regularly to your family members back home. When someone back home is sick, wants to go to school, or needs clothing, it will be regarded as being your responsibility. Some relatives may be genuinely sick, but others pretend to be sick so that you will send them some money. If you do not send money, because you suspect that they are playing games, and someone dies; you will have that person's death on your conscience for the rest of your life. You don't want that, and if you do not have the money, you will be prepared to borrow it from a friend to help your relatives. Some of these people are your brothers, your sisters, your cousins, your nephews, your nieces, your partner's relatives, and do not forget that one day you will have your own kids.

In Africa, if there is no room left in your house, some of these people end up sleeping in your kitchen or living room or in the corridor, as long as they can find a space to lay their bodies and sleep. These people will use the electricity and water, which means your utility bills will increase, and you will also incur additional costs because you are feeding them. If one of them is sick, it will be your responsibility to take him or her to the hospital and pay for any prescriptions. These people who live in your kitchen, your living room, and your corridor will make babies, and because they live in your house; you will take care of their babies as well as their partners. What can you do? Kick them out and have the furore of all your family against you? You cannot afford to have your brothers, sisters, aunties, uncles, and partner accusing you of being selfish, hypocritical, nasty, malicious, and ungrateful. You cannot afford to be isolated. Africa is about family, togetherness. Those who work must help those who are not working. You were born into that system and will die in that system whether you want to or not.

We have few jobs available in Africa; even if you are the right person for the job, you need to pay for the job or you will never be hired. Sometimes you spend a lot of money on a job, but you still do not get that job, and you cannot get your money back because the crooks who have your money know some police officers or a judge somewhere and there is nothing you can do. Every job has a price. The right jobs are given to the wrong people, and because they can afford it, they will always find any job of their choice. If you can afford to pay, you will work; if not, you will remain unemployed for the rest of your life. That is the situation in Africa, where poor but intelligent young men and women waste their knowledge and talent because they do not have the financial means to pay for a job in their field after they graduate.

If you are lucky enough to have a job, with so many relatives dependent on you, you cannot have a decent living. If you die without any savings for your family, then the standard of living your own children will have becomes uncertain. And if you survive but have only a low income, you cannot provide better living conditions for your immediate family because you are also working to take care of your relatives' children. How much must an African employee earn to pay the living expenses of so many dependants? How much must an African person who lives in Europe earn to take care of all his extended family members left in Africa? Given his situation, how do you expect an African employee in Africa not to be corrupt? Even the most honest, devoted, frank, straightforward, open human being would become corrupt. The temptation to make some extra money on top of your salary at the end of the month will be too great to resist. It is easy to have rules and regulations against corruption, but anyone in that situation with that system would become corrupt. Imagine two employees working for the same company with the same salary in Africa. One of them is honest and incorruptible and depends only on their salary on which to live. The other is corrupt and is always looking for any way to top up their monthly salary. The corrupt employee will have a much better life than the honest employee. If the two are friends, other people – especially members of the honest one's family – will wonder how he or she cannot manage to have the same lifestyle as his or her friend, knowing that they have the same job and the same salary. The honest one's own family will criticize him or her for neglect. No matter how honest you are, you will be forced into corruption, and there is nothing you can do. Corruption is present at every level of society in Africa, from the President to the lowliest man of the population. In Africa, the higher the status of the job you do, the more money you can make through corruption. In these conditions, almost anyone would do the same to top up their salary at the end of the month. You cannot blame employees in Africa for being corrupt; the system forces them to be the way they are.

To cut out corruption, you must fulfill certain conditions before you can have children. These conditions are:

You must be married and be at least eighteen years old. Education can help reduce underage pregnancies.

One of the parents must have a job and be able to regularly provide food, clothes, and pocket money for each child.

You must have a place of your own, whether you own it or rent it.
Both parents must be able to love the child without any doubt, regardless of the sex and the physical state of the child.

Each month, a certain amount of money (to be decided by the government) must be put into the account of each child. The child will use the money when he or she is old enough and ready to start his or her own family. Some of that money could be used for the child's healthcare and his or her education.

Why should anyone have to pay for someone else's pleasure?

We cannot stop people from having sex, but we can punish them for bringing a child into this world when they are not prepared mentally, emotionally, physically, and financially to take care of that child. If something happens to a child, though, a full investigation must be carried out to find out who is responsible.

This law must not be used to discriminate against any ethnic, religious, tribal, or caste minority group. We must not refuse work to certain people to stop them from having babies. For this system to work, the government must create enough jobs and give the same opportunity to every citizen in the country. The government must provide strong financial help for families that are finding it difficult to bring up their children.

For example, the government can top off each child's bank account for families of low income, especially when the breadwinner dies before the child is old enough to earn his own living.

Children from different backgrounds (rich or poor) must be given the same opportunity to succeed in life.

Each government must have a strong policy against bullying, harassment, xenophobia, racism, and abuse of power at work. What is the point of having rules and regulations when these rules and regulations are not enforced properly? What is the point of having rules and regulations when some people think they are untouchable, that they can do whatever they want, just because they know somebody at the top? When you are the one who is the victim in that situation, there is nothing you can do because of fear of losing your job. Nobody must be above the law.

For Defence

We do not need an army to defend a useless president. We do not need an army to defend a corrupt government. An army must not be used to oppress its own people. We have an army to defend the country and its population. To protect a stable country and a strong economy, one needs a strong army. There must be a system in which the best men and women are promoted. It is vital to avoid any discrimination and any xenophobia in an army. A frustrated person with a gun in his hands is very powerful and very dangerous. Leaders cannot fill the army with their family members and friends because they are scared of a coup. A national army and police must have its best men and woman in its higher ranks: those who are patriotic.

Being patriotic is priceless. You cannot change sides from government forces to rebel forces during a civilian war in your country because rebel leaders are promising you more money or a higher rank in their army if they win the war against your country. You have to be the most stupid human being on this planet to believe that rebels will promote you after the war. They always have their own people for any job if they get control of the country. You cannot call yourself patriotic when you can be bought by rebels to fight against your country. If you are patriotic, you will die patriotic. You must refuse to follow rebel ranks even if they give you all the money on the planet. You must die patriotic, side by side with the national army, even if you have to do it without waiting for any reward. Your mother country is crying out for help. If your country has been attacked by savages who have gone on a killing spree, you do not need to ask whether to defend your country. It's a natural instinct to protect and defend your motherland at any cost when that land is violated.

The army must be full of those who are willing to die for their country, for their people. You cannot just be in an army because you need a job. There are some jobs to be done: to protect and serve your country even if it means death, and you have to do it with honour, dignity, courage, love, and pride. Make sure the army is well equipped and well prepared mentally and physically to do its job. The aerial space, coastline, and land of the country must be under surveillance 24/7. Therefore, you need to provide all the technology your army needs for the sake of your people and the stability of your country. We can seek help from China, Russia or some of the other Eastern countries if the West is too expensive for technology, training, and maintenance of the equipment used in the army.

During war, the brave men and women who die defending the integrity, prestige, and honour of their countries must be remembered forever. Each year these brave soldiers who died or fought defending their countries, their families must be honoured. Their children must be helped financially, emotionally, so that they will not feel the absence of these brave soldiers.

We can organize our army using the same structure as America, England, or Canada. Members of the national army (no matter the rank they occupy) must not be allowed to support or defend any political party in public. Soldiers are not allowed to engage in politics or defend any political leaders, no matter what.

The army must stay neutral, no matter the rank a soldier occupies.

Mind-set of African leaders

The whole world judges African people through the eyes of their leaders. Most of these leaders, are in power in their respective countries because of the Western financial, military and political power and not chosen by African people. These African leaders see European, Chinese, and other super power countries as semi-gods. African leaders believe and trust their semi-gods more than themselves and their own people. A white person can commit the most outreach crime in Africa and nothing will happen to that person. No investigation, no punishment, nothing. The police will let him go. In contrast, a black person can be humiliated, harassed, raped, sent to prison for a crime he/she did not commit and no African leaders will demand answers.

When an African becomes rich, the money made in Africa is sent to the European banks or invested in Europe (buying houses, shares in some company etc.). His children are sent to Europe to study or to live in Europe. When the new rich are sick, they run as fast as possible to go to any European countries to use the health services. And when they die, the body is sent back to Africa, to their respective countries. Africa is not a cemetery.

For the economy

There are two different types of business that can affect the way people live in these countries: African and Europe Europeans countries' businesses are based on competence and a free market, in contrast to African countries' businesses driven by connection and corruption.

–   In Europe for example, a business person can have financial help, and guidance from its government. When that business person makes money he/she can invest that money in another business to create more work for the people of that particular country. A business person can plan in years and watch that business grow. He/she does not have to worry about any government that will be in place in that particular country. No matter who comes to power in any European country, the opposition or ruling government, there is always continuity. The work of the last government is finished by the next government.

–   In Africa, by contrast, for a business person to make it or to make a big profit instantly you must be close to somebody in power. That person can be a relative, a friend, or a friend of a friend. When these people in business in that particular country in Africa make money, that money is taken away and invested to another country in Europe just in case the power changes. These types of businesses based on connection are fragile because you do not know what the future holds. If the person you know in the higher place in the current government loses his power or is out of office, you do not know what will happen to your business. Especially when the new person in power is not someone you know or he/she is not from your religious or ethnic group. In these types of situation, the minute you make money you have to protect your assets. In that market, volatile environmental things can change in a second and you as a business person will not have enough time to protect your future. That is why businesses in Africa cannot compete with Western businesses. That is the reason African countries are poorer. Our leaders in Africa and their followers are taking money in their respective countries. Instead of investing that money to create more jobs for the population, that money is reinvested in Europe, Canada, America. African leaders and their followers starve their respective countries economically and make European countries richer. That money invested in Europe is then given to African countries as a loan with massive interest rates. A business based on connection and corruption forces the best brains in the country to leave. These smart people do not want to waste their intelligence, because they want to use their intellect to make money; and not be kissing the asses of some officers in the government to make a living. Top talents will go where their talent will be rewarded and appreciated.

Any African leaders do not need to go to European countries and borrow enormous some of money, unless these African leaders, their colleagues and family members use their new position to get rich as much as possible. A good leader needs to organise his/her country. You need to know which companies (big or small) pay the correct taxes and which don't. This is where you need to be brutal against corruption. A good leader must do everything in his/her power to fight corruption. When a company needs to pay, for instance one thousand dollars annually in taxes and someone (government officers) through corruption gets three hundred dollars, the company involved keeps seven hundred dollars. The country in this case loses seven hundred dollars. It's a lot of money that has been lost. Imagine when this type of corruption occurs in the country. Imagine how much money the country has lost when all the companies that operate in the country are put together? That money if well collected can be used to build schools, hospitals, roads, factories and many other things to develop the country.

What African leaders need to know is that European banks were created to make money. When a big or small bank gives any African country money, that money must be paid back with a huge interest rate.

For all the employees in the country, as a respected government you need to make sure when your citizen worked; no matter what kind of job they do, it's the legitimate duty of the employers to pay the employees. Any government needs to impose a minimum wage structure so that employees will not be exploited, abused and used like slaves. Without law and order, employers will pay their employees when they want and how they want. Employees work every month or sometimes for a year without any wages. How will these employees feed their family? How will these employees take their children to school? How will these employees pay for hospital bills, electricity bills and water bills? How can these employees have a normal, decent life as any human being in their own country? A country well organised, where the government knows how many of its citizens work and how many of its citizens do not have a job, that government can have an idea about how much it spends on wages and how much money it gets in return in the waged taxes.

In order for a country to be economically independent, it needs its own currency. You do not need to be an expert in economy to know that.

African countries must choose three countries on this planet that have the best economies – countries like the United Kingdom, America, and Japan. Copy the example of these countries, such as how employees are paid, how the tax system is designed, how the banks work, how much food costs, and how much cosmetic products cost. Try to make sure the lifestyle of the citizens of these countries is the same as the lifestyle of your citizens. Make sure we do not copy their past mistakes, especially the mistakes those banks made to cause the recession in Europe, America, and Asia in the year 2009.

How the currency needs to be designed. Example

- One coin of one dime
- One coin of two dime
- One coin of five dime
- One coin of ten dime
- One hundred dime makes one coin or one note of your country's money
- One note of 5 of your country's money
- One note of ten of your country's money
- One note of twenty of your country's money

Money need to be designed similar to that in England.

The power of the economy depends on the spending strength of the population. I'm amazed how European countries, such as the United Kingdom, organize their economic systems. If one goes to a typical supermarket, one can see rich, poor, and working-class families buying the same food and the same goods at the same prices. The only way one can tell if a person next to you in a queue is rich or not is waiting to see if they are going home by bus or driving an expensive car. European countries have stronger economies than African countries because the West allows each adult person to have the basic conditions to live: enough money to pay for food, pay bills, send their children to school, and pay the rent. Healthcare is available to everybody, rich or poor. All this is possible because there is stability, democracy, and enforcement of law and order; you are presumed innocent until proven guilty in a court of law, no matter how rich or poor you are. Stability and democracy brings investment. Private or foreign companies are comfortable investing in these countries because nobody will force them out as long as they observe the law. These companies are not afraid to invest in these countries because nobody will stage a coup to replace a government. These companies are happy to invest in these countries because they know they can make profits without being forced to bribe some government official to gain some unnecessary advantages over their rivals. Corruption is everywhere, even in Europe. The difference between African and European countries is that in Africa you can smell, touch, see, and eat corruption. Anything you want to do, you must bribe someone. Many Africans are not that bothered by bribery. For them it is a normal part of life. This attitude is exhibited even if the stability, the honour, the prestige, or the security of the country is at stake. People just don't care as long as they can make some money. These companies could create jobs, reduce crime, and allow the economy to grow.

Western countries create a system in which rich people become richer and poor people have opportunities to become rich. In Africa, our so-called leaders create a system in which rich people are becoming poor; therefore, to keep their wealth, they must steal more, and poor people become 'mad animals' willing to do anything, even the unthinkable, for a handful of cash. Moral values do not exist as long as they can make some money to survive.

How to eradicate poverty in Africa:
- You need stability and peace. Without stability no country in this world will progress, no matter the genius, the hard work and the talent of the government in charge of the country.
- Law and order.
- Good organisation of the country administration.

Any serious government needs:
- To know who paid taxes and who do not.
- A minimum wage system must be implemented so that employees cannot be abused and exploited like slaves.
- To know how many people are employees (private and public sector). They are people who are not officially employees but have their wages paid every month and that is corruption at the higher level. Any serious government cannot afford to lose money like that. Knowing the number of employees in your country allows any government to know how much money is used to pay the wages of employees and how much money is left. That money can be used to

invest where it is needed the most, like building hospitals and roads.

- Punish severely these who do not pay their employees correctly or on time or those companies who refuse to pay the amount of money in taxes their companies owe the government.
- Any ambassador in Europe can make a lot of money for the corresponding countries. Do not rely on visa fees only. There is so much each ambassador can do for their citizens when the country is well-organised, well-structured and law and order is implemented. For each African child born in a foreign country, that child needs to be registered in each corresponding embassy (a fee will be paid). For those Africans who live in Europe or America and would like to invest in their countries of origin – for example: you want to transfer money from your bank account in Europe to your bank account to your country in Africa. You live in Europe and want to buy a house, land or build a house in your country in Africa. These are opportunities African countries can use to make money for their respective countries, knowing that there are some reasonable fees that will be paid. To be successful any government must have the power, the courage, the desire to investigate and punish any kind of wrong doing or corruption. Any investments, small or big, must guarantee by the corresponding government of any African countries, and be prepared to reimburse any citizen money when he/she is not satisfied. Those people who have the responsibility to invest the money of those Africans who live in Europe must be well-trained, well-educated and trustworthy. In each embassy those employees who have the duties to help their citizens, must have business minds to help, guide and advise their respective citizens. The embassy employees who are doing a very good job must be

rewarded, honoured and those who have that kind of mind like: 'I do not care or it's not my money' and do very bad jobs must be named, shamed and sacked from their jobs and the money lost must be taken from those have taken it and given back to the owner in full. Any investment must well documented, signed by both parties (the ambassador employee and the citizen). The paperwork must be done in a civilized way so that it can be easier to trace those responsible, in case there are any complaints. Instead of borrowing huge sums of money from the IMF (International Monetary Fund), each African country must rely on its own ideas and own initiatives to make money. How would you expect the world to respect you as a nation when you portray Africans countries as eternal beggars, African countries always beg, always take, but they never give. Each year millions of African people want to invest in their countries of origin, but because of the lack of trust they are very scared to invest. Those who are brave enough to invest, see their investment stolen and there is nothing you can do about that. The police are corrupt, the justice system is disorganised and corrupt. Any complaint is a waste of time and waste of money. No one wants to hear you or investigate to find out those responsible. Any government cannot mislead and steal from its citizens.

–   Ambassadors for each country need to know how many of its citizens live in foreign countries and be able to intervene in each family issue in trouble; the same way couples' issues are solved in Africa. It is vital for couples to be together for the safety, security, progress and stability of the child. A man and a woman need to know how to respect, obey, help and support each other. Africans have their culture and tradition and a man has his duty and role to play and also a woman has her duty and role to play in a family. A life of a child from a broken family is bleak, especially when that child lives in Europe or America. No African child must be left behind. Any African child born in any European country or in America is part of the society of that country. That child has the same rights as any white child in that European or American country. An African child born in Europe or America must be given all the support, and a lot of love from his mother and from his father. An African child growing up in a very solid family-oriented way has a very good chance to succeed in life. That child can be a doctor, a pharmacist, a businessman or businesswoman, an entrepreneur, a politician, an engineer. That child can use his experiences, his connections, his financial power to bring some very good opportunities to his country of origin. The country of origin of that child can take full advantage of his knowledge. The main rule is that when you as an African live in Europe, you will never make it on your own. A man needs a woman and a woman needs a man, and together you form a team and life becomes easier, more comfortable and manageable. You cannot force a man and woman to live in a toxic relationship. A toxic relationship is a relationship where there is violence, bullying, manipulation, threat, is controlling, has lack of trust and intimidation. That kind of relationship is not a safe place to raise a child and if both parents decide to separate; both parents must be wise enough to find a common ground to make sure the interests of their children is their number one priority. Both parents must do whatever is needed to safeguard their child's well-being by putting in place a structure where the child can see, talk and visit both their parents when necessary. Children must not be used as a weapon to take revenge or hurt each other.

- Create some job centres where companies will go to recruit employees. Job centre officers must be professional, well-trained to avoid any type of xenophobia and discrimination. Job centre officers must read the contract to make sure companies will not exploit their employees: very low paid or no paid, sick leave, pension, annual leave, how many hours a week an employee must work a week and health care if the employees are sick or if female employees are pregnant.

For the Health System:

When you take as an example countries like Germany, Holland and the United Kingdom, the health system must be organized like their health systems. We need to have the same laboratories:
Hematology, Biochemistry, Histology, Cytology, Virology, Immunology, Microbiology, cardiology, rheumatology etc. We must train men and women who are well-equipped intellectually to maintain the equipment and know how to use them properly. We need to have the same structure as their hospitals: how their hospitals are organized, how many people they hire in each department and each ward, how much they are paid monthly, and what qualifications are required to do these jobs. We need to create a system in which the best employees are promoted, and severely punish those who sexually harass women. We must learn about their past mistakes and how to avoid them. Each government must be able to provide good healthcare to each citizen. It's a necessity, not a luxury.

For Communication

Ignorance is like a cancer, a virus we Africans must eradicate from our people. People should know how their country is run, and by whom. Africans need to know who is working well for the nation and how to reward them and who is stealing from them and how to punish them, regardless of their ethnicities, tribes, or caste groups or the posts they occupy. People should put their country first. The people also need to know their legitimate rights and duties. All African people need to learn how to read and write. They need to know how to love themselves and their countries. We Africans are tired of fighting amongst ourselves, fighting each other's ethnic groups, tribes, or religious war, usually for trivial reasons. To achieve that goal, we have to ensure our people are educated. No matter how rich you are, no matter how poor you are, no matter how talented you are in a chosen sport, no matter how attractive or unattractive you are, a black person without education is less than a human being. A black person without education is a savage. Through education, African people can FREE their minds. Education must be our best and biggest weapon against racism, poverty, ignorance, superstition, myths, xenophobia, rebellion and coups. Education allows you to understand how the world works, it teaches you to resist being used by politicians for their greed. Without education you expose yourself to being humiliated, harassed, intimidated, violated and used like chewing gum. Through education you can have a chance for a job and to improve your living conditions.

Once you have a job, a man needs a woman or a woman needs a man. If you are a man and want to get married it is important to get a woman who is educated, ambitious and above all, who is not lazy. Imagine, just imagine after your hard work, you have a job and get married based on the beauty of the lady who believes because you are a man it is you duty to pay all the bills in the house. The man is the head, according to African culture, but it does not mean you have to pay for everything. You cannot on your own pay for the gas bill, electricity bill, the rent or mortgage. Because your wife is not working you have to pay for your own mobile phone, your wife's mobile phone and the home phone. Added to that you will have children who will need food, toys, clothes, holidays. To be able to have a decent life you need a woman who can help you share the bills in the house. It is the same for a woman. Women need men who can help them to improve their living conditions. Once you can save, the extra money can be invested in your children's education. You can pay for extra learning lessons to give your kids an advantage to have very good grades. We live for our children and as a parent you wish that your children's life must be better than ours. We must do whatever it takes to get out of the poverty and to do that as a man you must choose your woman carefully. A woman who is prepared to work hard and who is not lazy. On your own it's always difficult, but two people working together makes life so much easier.

Unless African people FREE their minds, they will never be free.

If any government creates any policies allowing a strike to disrupt your education, that government is your worst enemy, and therefore you have the power to evict those responsible. They stop your education while their children are in the best universities in Europe. You cannot accept that.

Africans need to be informed of what's going on, not only in Africa but also in the rest of the world. Our people need to know how other people on this planet see us, specially the West. Why they judge us in the negative way that they do, and what to do to change that negative perception of us.

Not all African people are thieves, rapists and gangsters. Africans are not all lazy, ugly, uneducated, drug dealers, violent and rude. Among African people there are good, decent, hard-working people. Among African people there are intelligent, educated, good-mannered, openminded, pleasant and beautiful people.

Africans need freedom of expression, freedom of speech and freedom of religion without fear of persecution. People in Africa need to know how Africans lead their lives in Europe. We do not need lies; we need the truth, nothing but the truth. It's easy to pretend life in Europe is easy for everyone, when we Africans who live in Europe know it is not as easy as we thought it would be. Life in Europe is better than that in any African country because there is stability in Europe. There are more job opportunities. In Europe we now live in peace (people don't live in fear of a coup, or of a civil war at any time), and law and order is enforced. If you work you know you will get your wages at the end of the month.

The constitution of each African country must forbid any political party to own a newspaper. The journalists and the press must be free from interference; they must be impartial. The press must be in private hands and carry out their role according to internationally accepted norms of high-quality journalism. If different political parties have their own newspapers, they use them to start attacking each other, pushing and mentally preparing their respective members to go to war. Irresponsible leaders use these strategies very often to start a civil war.

Journalists must be able to do their jobs without fear of persecution of them, their friends, or their families. Take as an example the European press, how they do their jobs, the laws to protect them, and how they are organized.

If any government refuses to apply the Bangne Plan, the army must follow these steps:

1. The armed forces must gather and create a committee. That committee has a duty to ensure that the army is united as one patriotic institution that cares for the nation and for the well-being of its people regardless of ethnic, tribal, caste, or religious background. What must be avoided is a situation where one part of the army supports a government because the head of the army is related to the president through ethnicity, tribe, caste, or religion. Once everybody in the army, irrespective of rank, is united, the army may take power in a coup.
2. The press must be free and privatized to do their jobs. Use as an example how the press is organized in Western countries like England, Germany or Holland. The people need to be informed of what's going on in their country and in the rest of the world.
3. The senators must be elected according to the Bangne Rules.
4. Each political party, no more than eight in each country, must have their ministers ready according to the Bangne rules. Each minister for each ministerial department must gather his staff together to create a new structure for each department. These departments must be organized based on the Western model, and they must create a new constitution. The new constitution must be based on the constitutions of three European countries while taking into account our traditions and culture. Any law that is in contradiction with our way of life and our traditions and culture must be rejected.
5. The committee must invest in a new army and police that are strong, organized, patriotic, and wellequipped to serve and protect its motherland. Without security,

nothing is achievable. Then the army must surrender power within a year of the coup by organizing a free and fair election where the people are free to choose the best candidate. Democracy and stability: this is all we need. Any greedy army leaders who refuse to hand over power to the people by giving them the opportunity to elect their president must be punished by the people. No matter how strong you are, no matter how powerful your army is, no matter how smart you are, no matter how rich you are, when the people decide enough is enough; there is nothing you can do to stop them.

Conclusion

Africa is not a paradise for paedophiles, where these evil people can come and do whatever they want with our babies – things they would not dare do in their own countries. Africa is not a no-man's land where anybody (criminal or rich) is free to do or buy whatever they want without fear or worry of prosecution because as long as they have money, they can buy the law when it suits them. Africa is not a dustbin that rich countries can fill with their chemical waste or take what they want free of charge. We Africans must show to the world and to ourselves that we are not savages, that we do not live in a jungle with wild animals but are human beings like them. We Africans need to work as hard as them to improve our way of life like they did.

I dream that one day all African countries will be as powerful as Western countries: peaceful, prosperous, and stable. I dream, just dream, that one day in each country in Africa, in each village, in each town, and in each province, Muslims, Christians, and followers of other religions will live together in peace, harmony, love, and respect for each other's religions. I dream of African countries where all the ethnic, tribal, or castes groups will be mixed through marriages in peace, harmony, and love to break these prejudices of high or low ethnic, tribal or caste descent. I dream that one day each country in Africa, each village, each town, and each province, will be run by an honest, fair, just man or woman who will fear God and be willing to put the lives and well-being of the people before his or her own life. I dream of African countries where one day the lion and the sheep will be able to drink water from the same river, side by side, without any fear or worry. That dream is impossible right now, but what is now impossible can become achievable. We Africans cannot be eternal parasites who, without the help of the West, are destined for certain death. Our future and the future of our children is in our hands. We Africans must sweat blood if necessary; we must sacrifice our lives to make sure our children, our grandchildren and our great-grandchildren can live in our motherland with peace, prosperity, stability, love, and pride. We must do whatever is needed to allow our children, grandchildren, and great-grandchildren to have a better life than ours and not be forced to leave their motherland to find a better life elsewhere.

How do you feel as a parent when you cannot afford to feed your children regularly? What kind of life do you have as a parent when you cannot afford to take your children to the hospital, no matter how minor the injuries are? What kind of human being are you when you are forced to live in shanty houses without electricity and running water in this day and age while your so-called leaders are piling up your money in foreign bank accounts? How do you feel when you cannot afford a decent education for your children while your leaders are sending their children to the most expensive schools or universities in Europe? What kind of life do you have when you have no rights, when you are humiliated and ignored in your own country? How do you feel when you and your family are forced to be refugees in your own country because of a religious or ethnic war? How do you feel when your army is too weak and too corrupt to protect you and your family from those who would harm you during a civil war? Are you going to sit there hoping that God will come to do something about these injustices, or are you going to fight for your children, your grandchildren, and your great-grandchildren?

In a country where there is no stability and no democracy, where law and order are not enforced, anything can happen.

Today leaders, their associates, and their families are in 'heaven' while the majority of the population are living in 'hell'.

Tomorrow, with the help of a foreign power, somebody will replace them peacefully or by force and the new leaders, their associates, and their families will be in 'heaven' while the majority of the population – including the former leaders, their associates, and their families – will be living in 'hell'. What goes around comes around.

Is this the kind of life you want for your children, your grandchildren, and your great-grandchildren?

Our traditional way of life was cut short by Western culture during the period of slavery. We Africans envied the West because of their technology, their architecture, and their way of life, but technology and buildings are not everything in life. The way that Western people live their lives is not necessarily always the best way. We must learn how to cultivate and maintain our moral values. If we want to be competitive and strong in this twenty-first century and beyond, we Africans must merge both cultures (African and Western), select the very best aspects from each culture, and make a new African culture.

Anyone who attacks my country is my enemy.

Anyone who collaborates with the enemy of my country is my enemy.

THE END